Live the Life

Many are the words we speak,
Many are the songs we sing,
Many kinds of offerings,
But now to live the life.

Matt Redman

Live the Life

a *soul survivor* guide to doing it

Mike Pilavachi

with Craig Borlase

Hodder & Stoughton
LONDON SYDNEY AUCKLAND

British Library Cataloguing in Publication Data
A record for this book is available from the British Library

ISBN 0 340 78591 8

Typeset by Avon Dataset Ltd, Bidford-on-Avon, Warks

Printed and bound in Great Britain by
The Guernsey Press Co. Ltd, Channel Islands

Hodder and Stoughton
A Division of Hodder Headline Ltd
338 Euston Road
London NW1 3BH

To Bishop David Pytches
mentor, father, friend

Contents

Acknowledgments   ix
Foreword   xi
Introduction   1

Part I Getting Ready
1 Making friends with God   5
   (it all begins with friendship)
2 There was a donkey, a nun and a Greek bloke . . .   18
   (a chapter about worship)
3 Tea, toast and tortoises   33
   (a chapter about prayer)
4 God whispers to his friends   46
   (a chapter about listening to God)

Part II Getting Steady
5 The yeast in your beer   61
   (this one's about faith)
6 Chocolate and other evils   74
   (a chapter about temptation)
7 Everybody loves a lover   88
   (a chapter about being family)
8 I am a five-cow woman   104
   (a chapter about self-image)
9 Learning to catch   119
   (a chapter about healing)

Part III Go

10 Why I left Harrow   135
    (a chapter about evangelism)
11 Go   149
    (another chapter about evangelism)
12 How far should we go?   162
    (being part of the culture)
13 Where should we go?   171
    (what is your calling in life?)
14 Does God take Visa?   184
    (a chapter about generosity)
15 How to keep on going   196
    (a chapter about persevering)

Acknowledgments

We would like to thank a number of our friends who have helped us in the writing of this book: Elspeth Taylor, who had the original idea and has been a constant encouragement since; Andi Smith and Dave Baxter, who so accurately typed the transcripts; Andrew Latimer, for help and advice well beyond the call of duty; Matt Redman, David Pytches, Emma Mitchell, Mark Stibbe, Martyn Layzell and Emily Trotter, who read the manuscript and made many wise and helpful comments. We would like to thank Emma Borlase, who is wife to one of us and friend to both, and whose thoughts can be found by the discerning in various parts of this book. Last but not least, we would like to thank our church, Soul Survivor Watford. Many of the thoughts and ideas in this book have been learned in this community and many of the stories are about you. Sorry.

Foreword

You've been to the festival, got the CD and bought the t-shirt. Well, now . . . here's the book. Soul Survivor – what can one say? – it's an event, a series of celebrations, a local church, a radio show. But don't be fooled, for more than anything else Soul Survivor is really just a bunch of people. I suppose 'just' is not quite right, for God has clearly been using Mike and the people working alongside him in some incredible ways.

Live the Life is a meaty, beaty, big and bouncy book – good description of the author I would say. Mike Pilavachi has crammed this one full of down-to-earth and practical advice about being a Christian. Here we get behind the inevitable hype and distance which goes with any large event and we get to peep inside the soul of Soul Survivor.

Mike has laid out in some detail what makes him tick, and from beginning to end it is an amazing story of intimate encounter with God. Sounds serious, and it is, but along the way there are a good many laughs. Look out for the spiritual significance of chocolate cake and Mike Tyson's taste for ears.

Live the Life is an excellent book for those starting out in the Christian life and I recommend it to you. For those who may want to know more about Mike and the ideas behind the festival (and of course all those other activities – did I mention the magazine?) this book is a must. *Live the Life* reveals a refreshing depth of spiritual and theological insight which is often not associated with crowd-pulling charismatic youth work.

> Pete Ward – The Archbishop of Canterbury's
> Adviser for Youth Ministry

Introduction

Something is happening in the Church. It used to be that young people were fighting to get out; today they're coming back. Everywhere we go we see a generation with a new passion for Jesus, we see a generation that's rising up with a radical commitment to living the life. This book is written to encourage all those who want to go deeper with God and further out into the world.

Because preparation is everything, *Live the Life* tries to help with the business of getting to grips with the hows and the whys of Christian living. Taking it in three practical chunks, we first of all sink our pre-molars into getting ready: looking at the roots of our relationship with God. Then we move on to examine how we make sure we're steady, both in ourselves and in our relationships with others. Finally we rinse out with a look at the ways we can respond to a simple instruction: Go.

This book is best read with a Bible near by. As you find Scriptures weaving in and out you will want to check them for yourself. We need to get God's teaching into every aspect of our lives.

God is calling his people to go beyond the caramel coating of life. The need today is for people who will want to meet with him and who will want him to reach every aspect of their lives. Worship and obedience are good words, fine qualities for us to take on. If our worship takes us deeper with God, it will take us further out into the world, obeying him with all our lives.

Mike Pilavachi
Craig Borlase
January 1998

Part I
Getting Ready

1

Making friends with God

(it all begins with friendship)

I got out my ruler and drew a thick red line underneath the title 'Why I am not a Christian'. I had just spent 600 words annihilating one of the five major world religions, and I felt good. The way I saw it, Christianity was for the old, the weak and the stupid. My essay explained it all perfectly clearly, and anyone who read it would be forced to:

1 agree
2 say that I was a fourteen-year-old genius, and
3 give me an A+ and let me off cross-country for the rest of the term.

Things didn't go quite as I planned, and I later found out that forty years before me someone else had also written an essay with the same title, but his was much better as he had a beard and was a philosopher called Bert. The other bizarre thing is that exactly one year after I had put pen to paper I decided to spend the rest of my life doing whatever Jesus wanted me to do. Being a Christian – I had discovered – was not about following a set of rules, but about something far more powerful and exciting: friendship.

Life begins with friendship. God decided that it would be good to share things, so he spent a busy six days in the workshop. Later, once we had managed to completely miss the point about God, Jesus came down to reunite us both. Finally the Holy Spirit was promised so that we might continue to be close to God, even after Jesus had been crucified, rose again and went to heaven. God wants us to be his friends. In John 15 verses 12 to 15, having just told the disciples that the Holy Spirit was on his way, Jesus says this:

> My command is this: Love each other as I have loved you. Greater love has no one than this, that he lay down his life for his friends. You are my friends if you do what I command. I no longer call you servants, because a servant does not know his master's business. Instead, I have called you friends, for everything that I learned from my Father I have made known to you.

The disciples were Jesus' friends. They weren't servants, slaves or paid companions, there to make him feel popular, they were all mates together. Friendship is nothing if we don't let people see what we're really like, and Jesus made sure that they knew everything that he had learned from his Father. He wept in front of them and told them about the things that made him happy and the things that made him sad.

The history of friendship

Friendship is a relationship. Way back when he was surrounded by lots of nothing, God decided to create the human race – people who would be like him – so that he could have relationship. He said, 'Let us make man in our own image, in our own likeness' (Gen. 1:26) and got on with the business of making someone he could love and be intimate with. Throughout the Old Testament we follow a story that has one main theme: God, the maker of heaven and earth, yearning for a relationship with Israel, the people that he had made a special pact with.

The arrangement we have that is most similar to the pact God made with Israel is marriage. Back then the people of

Israel agreed to love and obey their maker, and in return God would love, protect and care for them. This covenant was a unique agreement, but it broke God's heart as Israel was constantly falling short, turning away from a friendship with Almighty God. You see something of God's sorrow in the book of Hosea, where God told his prophet to marry a prostitute called Gomer. Hosea stuck by her and stayed faithful, but she carried on sleeping around (she lifted her skirt to every passing man). Hosea and God had something in common: the people they loved were not keeping their promises. God told Hosea to say to the nation that they were little more than a whore – unfaithful.

God's pain at this broken relationship was real, but he didn't leave it there. He sent Jesus to become like his creation so that his creation might once again become like him. Jesus became a man to take away the disease called sin which had separated us from friendship with God. By dying on the cross, Jesus told us that we can be forgiven, that we can be friends with God again. None of this would be possible if God didn't first love us, and our relationship is based on our response to God's love for us, as John was keen to point out:

Dear friends, let us love one another, for love comes from God. Everyone who loves has been born of God and knows God. Whoever does not love, does not know God because God is love. This is how God showed his love among us: He sent his one and only Son into the world that we might live through him. This is love: not that we loved God, but that he loved us and sent his Son as an atoning sacrifice for our sins.

(1 John 4:7–10)

Like the ceiling of the Sistine Chapel, where Michelangelo painted God's hand stretched out to touch ours, it is God who sets the ball rolling. Our role is to respond to his love, to the mercy he showed us when he sacrificed his Son. Our worship, our prayer, our reading of the Bible, our caring for the poor and our telling others about him all comes as a response to his call to us. Christianity is all about knowing Jesus and being children of the Father, knowing him through the forgiveness of his Son.

We see pictures of this all the way through the Scriptures. In John 17:3, in his great high-priestly prayer, Jesus says, 'Now this is eternal life: that they might know you, the only true God, and Jesus Christ, whom you have sent.'

Eternal life is not going to Mars and turning left, passing through a hole in the space/time continuum. Eternal life is about a relationship with God, and this physical life is all about getting to know each other beforehand. Bearing in

mind that this is why God made us, it is the most natural, normal thing that we as human beings can do. Because we were made by and for him, our worship is vitally important as it is an expression of our love for him.

A wonderful book in the Old Testament that works on the idea of this love relationship is the Song of Songs. Christians have found it hard to know what to make of it over the years, feeling that because it follows the progress of a love affair between two people, it might not be 'suitable' for the Church. It has been a bit of a favourite of mine, although at first I liked it just because it used the word 'breasts' more than once. Thankfully there is a bit more to it than snigger material for young boys, and it comes out as a great picture of the love affair between God and his people.

It is important to note that this is not a love affair of equals, that it's actually about a king and his maiden. In the same way we are not the equals of God. When we're called the friends of God, when the Bible calls the Church the bride of Christ, we are most definitely not the boss. After all, 'the friendship of the Lord is for those who fear him' (Ps. 25:14 NRSV). We have a friendship with Almighty God, not a pet poodle. In that way, knowing that God is boss takes the pressure off: for if the friendship depended on our being good enough, we'd all be very, very alone.

Yes, but God doesn't love me

This may all sound fine as a theory, but for many of us getting round to believing that God's love is for us is about as easy as believing that God has a bus pass. Look around you and there are plenty of examples of how God loves, cares and yearns for his people, but look inside and there's little more than a bad smell and a load of broken promises. If we've been Christians for a while we might have just about convinced ourselves that God loves us, but he only does it because he has to and, really, whenever he thinks of us he is totally unimpressed.

I love that passage where Jesus was baptised by John the Baptist and as he came out of the water the voice came from heaven saying, 'This is my Son whom I love; with him I am well pleased' (Matt. 3:17). Can you imagine how great it must have been to have God publicly shouting from the skies, 'This is my Son – I love him, I'm pleased with him.' Sometimes I go into a little fantasy and imagine myself with a group of people when all of a sudden God clears his throat and points his biggest and most God-like finger down at me.

'That Mike Pilavachi's all right,' he says, his booming voice shattering windows. 'I quite like him.'

Then I imagine how everyone's attitude to me would change. People would drop their shopping to point at me. 'Wow!' they would say, 'Mike Pilavachi, he's God's boy.' If that happened, I'd have t-shirts printed up that replayed the whole heavenly message every time I burped. Of course, the truly amazing thing is that it *has* happened (not the bit about the t-shirt): God has said he likes and loves me. Maybe it hasn't been quite the publicity stunt I would have planned, but through Jesus he said it loud and clear. Jesus didn't have to earn God's pleasure, and what God says about Jesus, his Son, he says about me and about you. God has said that he loves, likes and cares for each one of us.

Another reason lots of us have for finding it hard to believe in God's love is because our own experience of fathers has been rough. Lots of us find it hard to believe that God could be such a good friend because our friends have let us down. The solution to all this? We need to get deeply into the Bible, because in there we find the truth about God. As we read it we hear God speaking to us through the stories of his relationship with others. What's more, the Holy Spirit takes the words of the Bible and feeds them into our hearts, acting like a kind of high-grade spiritual fertiliser. That's why it's good to meditate on God's word, taking time to think over the words.

Believing that he does love me

One of my favourite passages to meditate on comes from a little book at the end of the Old Testament. It's one of the minor prophets, Zephaniah, but don't let that put you off.

> The Lord your God is with you, he is mighty to save,
> he will take great delight in you, he will quiet you with
> his love, he will rejoice over you with singing.
>
> (Zeph. 3:17)

In the past I've written it down and looked at it every day, feeding on the goodness it contains. I usually take it slowly, one line at a time:

> The Lord your God is with you

If you are a Christian, have given your life to Jesus and have made a commitment to him, then the Lord your God is with you. That means he isn't just there for you on Sundays, but the rest of the time too. When it gets to Monday morning and it's time to get back out there at school, college or work, it might be harder to feel, but it's true – he's with us. And not just tagging along, asking to be looked after . . .

> He is mighty to save

We need to remember that we have a powerful God with us, one who can make a difference to our lives. Imagine you and I are walking down a dark alley late at night on our own, and from the other end come a load of particularly violent-looking blokes. They stop us and ask what exactly it is that our eyes are focusing on. You're frightened and weigh up our chances. Four hard men against me, the pastor who cries whenever one of his pot plants dies. You do the only sensible thing and run away.

But imagine if you're walking down that dark alley with Mike Tyson at your side. Instead of staring at the floor and crossing your legs, you may have a bit of a swagger as the gang of four approach. If they asked if you wanted to make something of it, you might reply that, yes, you rather would. Then you could turn to Mike and tell him to eat as many of their ears as he wanted. God, in that situation, is more like Mike Tyson than Mike Pilavachi. God is mighty to save and big enough to make a difference in anybody's life. Whether it be saving us from our sins or stepping in with miracles or guidance, God has the power.

He will take great delight in you

By the time my meditation gets around to this bit I'm usually getting hungry. Strangely, this helps, as I take great delight in food so it gives me an idea of how God feels about me. Just like me when I'm served up a full Greek meal, God gets ecstatic when he thinks about us. He loves it when we meet together to worship him, and he loves it when we talk to him on our own. To know that God loves to hear my prayers is a great inspiration for me to pray. It helps me to know that he reacts to my prayers and makes me think of it as being a conversation.

He will quiet you with his love

I finally understood some of the meaning of this promise when I was browsing my way through the cheese section of my local supermarket. Somewhere around the Garlic Roule I saw a five-year-old boy looking miserable. Knowing that I didn't have much of a taste for garlic at the age I thought nothing of it and went back to my research. Soon he began to sniff and I realised what was going on. A lady came up to him and asked if he was lost. At that he started to bawl his eyes out, accompanying it with the sort of piercing sound that only five-year-old boys can make. Eventually an announcement came over the loudspeaker system: 'Would the mother of a little boy who answers to the name of "aaaaarh" please collect him from Soft Cheese.'

The boy's mum was soon there, cuddling him and telling him that everything was all right. The boy kept on crying but his mum kept holding, telling him that she loved him and wasn't going away. This carried on for some time until he stopped crying. She made him still, peaceful and secure again with her love. She quietened him with her love. Many of us may not cry on the outside like that five-year-old boy, but we've been so hurt and broken by things that have happened to us that we're crying on the inside. God says that he can be there for us. He will hold us and quiet us with his love.

He will rejoice over you with singing

I always thought it was our job to rejoice over him with singing, not his job to rejoice over us. Partly it's up to us to thank him for who he is and what he has done, but while we do that, he goes wild over us. The Hebrew phrase that translates as 'rejoice over you with singing' literally means 'to spin like a top and let out whoops of joy'. It amazes me that God does that for each one of us.

This verse from Zephaniah perfectly contains the message of Christianity. God is alive, forgiving, interested, compassionate, loving and worthy of praise. This is the

beginning of life. If we understand the truth of this, if we let it seep into our soul's roots, we will find ourselves living the most outrageously full life imaginable. If not, it's just all lifeless rules.

A few years ago I went on a trip to the Isle of Man to take some meetings. Matt Redman and I stayed with a family who had three boys, the youngest of whom was a six-month-old baby called Ben. As Matt, Ben and I sat at the dinner table waiting for the indigestion to fade, I was playing with Ben. Being a cuddly kind of guy I know all the moves, and I showed him my full repertoire. I bounced a little, made noises, hung him upside down and was balancing him on my chin when I sensed something brewing in his nappy region. Immediately I held him at arm's length, twisting my head this way and that to avoid the smell. My arms soon were starting to hurt so I passed him over to Matt. He rapidly sussed what was going on with the kid's butt, and before long he too was holding Ben as far away from his body as possible. Ben started to cry, unhappy at the combination of soggy nappy and stretched upper body. His mum came in and took hold of him, cuddling him as close to her as she could, unfazed by all the smell and mess he had created.

God, I realised, does exactly the same thing with us. When we're tired and miserable, unable to look after ourselves and having all sorts of hurts and problems, God pulls us in close. It's where he wants us; next to his heart.

Live it!

It's all very well nodding enthusiastically when we hear someone banging on about how important it is that we know how much God loves us, but just how deep does our knowledge of this go? What's more, why should we be bothering to worry about this sort of thing anyway? After all, isn't this just another case of Christians wanting to snuggle into Jesus and have him kiss it all better? The answer is 'no'. Try thinking about someone you know who is secure; not arrogant or brash, but secure and safe in the knowledge that they are valued by the people around them. How can you tell that they're secure? How do their lives tell the story? I've got a few people in mind, and in every case they're different because of what they *don't* do rather than what they *do*. They don't need to boast, to put others down, to worry about things full time or to push themselves to the front of the queue. Of course, there are many other traits we could pick up on, but just this handful gives us a hint of what being secure can do for us. Given that God's love and friendship is premium quality, doesn't it make sense that if we grow in the knowledge of God's love for us it will have some serious implications for the way we live our lives?

Task

What can you remember about the way Jesus behaved towards his disciples? Write down any examples you can think of that show how Jesus' words or actions communicated how he felt towards his disciples.

When you have done that, pick one of the gospels – Matthew, Mark, Luke or John – and work through it highlighting any example you can find where Jesus treats his disciples as friends. Look for what he says to them and what he does for them as well as how he helps them understand more of what the kingdom of God is about.

When you have finished take time to read through all the sections you have highlighted. Pause and meditate on these: let them build up a picture in your mind of how Jesus offered and delivered friendship. Turn back to Zephaniah 3:17, then read it, believe it and live it.

2

There was a donkey, a nun and a Greek bloke . . .

(a chapter about worship)

It's strange the way things change with the seasons. The summer of 1997 saw 10,000 people jumping up and down to a Country-and-Western-inspired tune, with lyrics that went, 'Na na na na na na, hey!' It was the soundtrack to that year's Soul Survivor festival, and as I watched the heaving hordes I asked myself a fundamental question: what on earth does this have in common with that old classic, 'All Things Bright and Beautiful'? Are they related? Can they really both be worship? What is worship, anyway?

According to the Bible, to worship our Father is our highest calling; nothing that we can do pleases God more. The Old Testament is full of examples of how, for the Israelites, the biggest battle was always who or what were they going to worship. There was never a question of whether they were going to worship; it was part of their nature – and the choice was always between worshipping God and worshipping idols. The bottom line for us today is exactly the same: the basic nature of humanity is to worship, so what are we going to focus on? For those of us who have chosen to worship the likes of New Labour, Manchester United, WWW or ourselves, there is but one antidote – to worship God.

The book of Jeremiah contains a potent verse in which God proclaims: 'My people have committed two sins. They have forsaken me, the spring of living water, and have dug their own cisterns, broken cisterns that cannot hold water'

(Jer. 2:13). This is the heart of the matter, the core of broken humanity: when we abandon God, turning away from relationship with him, we choose second best.

What is worship?

Worship is the ultimate expression of relationship with God. Worship is coming home. As the saying goes, within each of us lies a God-shaped hole – one that can be filled, not by a religious ritual, but only by a living relationship with him.

The word most often used in the New Testament for worship (sixty-six times in all) is the Greek word *proskuneo* – which literally means 'to come towards to kiss'. It means to come to a place of tenderness, to touch the heart of God and to allow him to touch our hearts. Worship is praise, worship is celebration, worship is intercession, but worship ultimately is adoration. As in the deepest of relationships, the most intimate place is the one where you can cherish and express your love for each other. The socialising, the chatting, all leads to the place of adoration. To worship God is our duty and is the greatest commandment that Jesus gave: love the Lord your God with all your heart, soul, mind and strength. To love him with all that we have and all that we are is the ultimate act of humanity.

The centuries-old Westminster Shorter Catechism was written in a question and answer format to give expression to the major doctrines of the Christian faith. Question number one gets stuck right in with 'What is the chief end of man?' Instead of replying that it is the head or the feet, the people let it rip with 'The chief end of man is to glorify God and enjoy him for ever.' This is our main function in life and presents Jesus' greatest commandment in another way: our object in life is to glorify God and enjoy him for ever – in other words, to worship.

How do we worship?

Thankfully (considering my innovative approach to vocal tuning) worship is more than just singing. Worship is about the whole of our life. If our songs and our instruments are doing one thing and our lives are doing another, it is a stench in God's nostrils. 'Away with the noise of your songs!' he says (Amos 5:23), if we are not living lives that match up to the words. Matching up the words and the lives is one heck of a big job; for if we are planning on adoring God, we are going to end up with a pretty long list of things to adore. At the end of the day worship cannot be separated from the marks of his character: justice, purity, mercy, compassion and truth. If we are going to have relationship with him we have to be prepared to explore the extreme breadth of his character, to find the ways of expressing his nature in every aspect of our lives.

One of the words used in the Old Testament for worship was the Hebrew verb which literally means 'to work'. Even today the Jews regard their work as part of worship – the whole of life is to be given over to him, not only what is done on the Sabbath or during prayer times but also what is done in the office or on the factory floor. Jesus illustrated this at the end of Matthew's gospel:

'I was hungry and you gave me something to eat, I was thirsty and you gave me something to drink, I was a stranger and you invited me in, I needed clothes and you clothed me, I was sick and you looked after me, I was in prison and you came to visit me.' Then the righteous will answer him, 'Lord, when did we see you hungry and feed you, or thirsty and give you something to drink? When did we see you a stranger and invite you in, or needing clothes and clothe you? When did we see you sick or in prison and go to visit you?'

The King will reply, 'I tell you the truth, whatever you did for the least of these brothers of mine, you did for me.'

(Matt. 25:35–40)

If we can learn to see worship as the way we relate to one another and not only to God while at church, we stand the chance of making real differences to the lives we come into contact with. When Mother Teresa was asked why she served the poor, she wrapped up the whole gospel with her answer: 'Because we love God.'

We will return to worship as a way of life later in the chapter, but for now let's look at worship in song. There seems to be a special place given in the Bible to God's people meeting together and worshipping with music. The Psalms are the Christian's handbook of this corporate worship. Many of the songs we sing today come straight from the Psalms. David wrote many of them as an act of worship that was to be put to music, expressing love, reverence, praise and thanksgiving to God, but without ignoring life's pain, confusion and questions. As well as being an expression of our desire to follow God and imitate his character through our deeds, worship is about bringing all these other things to God too. Often music is the ideal medium through which to express these complex emotions, because there is something about music that touches the human heart. If bands like Oasis can express the moods of our time through lyrics and attitude, then surely we too can use music to express a passionate love for God.

As an Afro-sporting teenager in North London my trips to the lower end of my mood swings were often accompanied by the music of Simon and Garfunkel. When they sang, 'I am a rock, I am an island,' I was there, belting it out with all the passion that my soul could muster. I had the words written out on a card and read them through

whenever I was feeling low. '*Yes*,' I'd say, 'that's how I feel: I touch no one and no one touches me.' The words became my chant, and even though this particular island *did* cry, this rock *did* feel pain, I sang them with all the passion in my soul. Whenever I hear it today I immediately find myself back in my room, with its orange and brown wallpaper, and me, ready to take on the world.

Another powerful aspect of music and worship is The Meeting. Way back when Solomon was king, overseeing the building of the temple, they had times when the musicians and the singers would get together and do their thing. The result was not some mildly relaxing mood-inducement – on the contrary, the glory of the Lord, his very essence, descended. It is important that the Bible notes that many people would take part in these times, because it reinforces the point made in Hebrews that we shouldn't neglect meeting together (Heb. 10:25) as each of us 'has a psalm, a hymn, a spiritual song' (Eph. 5:19) that we can contribute to the overall adoration of our Maker. The glory of the Lord descends when we offer ourselves to him in worship (see 2 Chron. 7). Even though it's confusing at times, it appears that the advice to 'not forsake meeting together' is pretty sound, and is worth sticking by. At Soul Survivor we have known times in our meetings when we have been worshipping God and suddenly have felt that his glory has descended. Not surprising, then, that many of us have been broken in times of worship. Because worship is all about relationship with God, it follows that the time we spend with him often results in him rubbing off on us, inspiring us to become more like him. In fact, it's often during the most intimate of moments that we can become inspired and feel the passion to do something practical, to worship through our lives.

But what if the meetings available to you aren't five-star worship bonanzas? Isn't it a little hard when the rest of the church doesn't understand and prefers things 'the old way'? Unfortunately there is a discipline in worship which many of us need to learn again. Often, when we have been involved in new and exciting things we forget that the songs themselves are unimportant; what matters is the heart. The decision to worship God whether we like the style or not is an act of spiritual discipline. The more alien we find the style, the greater the discipline.

Furthermore, we evangelicals seem to do a fairly good

job of keeping up with the Joneses when it comes to the secular world. These days it's marked by a mind-numbingly fast turnaround of style and information. What was 'in' last summer was probably 'out' by September, and what was news on a Monday was world-wide and fully downloadable by the time Monday's coffee was just beginning to get cold. Cultural relevance is another chapter, but as a pre-meal snack, try this: do we have to be slaves to the evolution of cool worship?

Worship is linked to a strange thing called anointing. Jesus was called the anointed one, and that literally means 'the Christ' in the Greek or 'the Messiah' in the Hebrew. To have an anointing for worship, as to have an anointing for healing, is in a sense to have something of Jesus there. At times worship can seem like a ritual, at the end of which you think it was technically good (they were in tune, in time or, depending on how fussy you are, were not wearing Lycra), but the people didn't touch the heart of God. The good piece of news, though, is that even if the rest of the congregation aren't engaging with God, there's nothing to stop us going for it. We are called to find Jesus in nature, in our meditations and among the poor – we surely ought to be able to find him in a church that worships in a different way.

What are the benefits of worship?

When we worship, we are healed. A version of a verse in Psalm 22 says the Lord inhabits the praises of his people; when we truly worship it is as if we are touching the heart of God. It reminds me of the woman who reached out to touch Jesus in the crowd, believing that if she could just touch the hem of his garment she would be healed. For me the most intimate of worship times gets me close to God, close enough that sometimes my own pain can be healed. The greatest emotional and spiritual healing has come when I have been worshipping God. I have wept before him in worship in a way I would never have done at any other time, and end up having found peace in my soul and feeling reorientated.

I once stood next to a nun at a meeting in Cockfosters. It was early days as far as what we would now call contemporary worship goes and, like the nun, I had travelled quite a way to reach that evening's meeting. It began with an introduction and was swiftly followed by the main event: 13.5 minutes of uninterrupted worship. Pure bliss. Song after song came at us – 'Joy is the Flag', 'Michael, Row Your Boat Ashore' – all done with the proper actions and everything. We hit the home straight running, turning out a particularly fervent rendition of 'Come Bless the Lord' that ended in a spontaneous round of applause. Man, we were on fire. Unfortunately the old nun must have been a little deaf, for she carried on clapping. She had this serene expression on her face, and I was just about to give her a shove when she stopped and looked around.

'I suppose you're all wondering why I carried on clapping?' she asked, blushing a little. 'You see, my hands have been paralysed with arthritis for years, but as we were worshipping I forgot all about it, and look – I'm healed!'

What the nun found out was that worship is about taking our eyes off ourselves and putting them on him. When we're not looking at ourselves, he sneaks in and heals us.

As well as healing us physically and emotionally, the Lord often speaks to us during times of worship, sometimes calling us to repentance. At one of the Soul Survivor meetings a whole queue of people formed at the front during the worship. Thinking they were about to complain, I was getting ready to apologise for the poor quality of the singer when the first one pulled out a knife. I contemplated making a run for it but realised they were younger and faster. I went closer and prepared to become Saint Mike Pilavachi, the Soul Survivor martyr.

'Can you get rid of this for me?' said Knife-boy.

I asked why (we Greeks are born with an acute sense of mistrust).

'God told me to,' he replied.

Then each of his friends came up and gave me their weapons. While I was obviously excited that God had done a wonderful thing in their lives, I must admit to feeling a little suspicious as to why they attended a Christian conference with enough weaponry to start a small military coup. For the rest of the week, whenever I passed them I made sure they kept their hands above their heads where I could see them.

How does worship relate to a church service?

As well as the worship time being a possible focus for repentance, healing and unity, it should also reflect and inspire the very direction in which the Church is moving. When the Vineyard movement started, the people would meet in a house, sing songs to Jesus and cry. They were people who were hurting, and who found that worship was the best way of carrying on a relationship with God. At Soul Survivor we feel similarly, and consider worship as our highest value and our first priority. It is neither the warm-up nor the wind-down: it is the main event.

Worship has always been at the heart of the church service, and at our church we try to keep the two walking in time with each other. Matt Redman has been our minstrel; we may have talked about a theme and the next thing you know he's written a song about it. Painful as it is for me to admit, I'm sure that God has taught more people through the songs than through my sermons; people don't sing my sermons in the shower, but they do sing the songs.

One example of this is Matt's song 'I'm Coming Back to the Heart of Worship'. We realised at Soul Survivor Watford, in the autumn of 1996, that we had got so into the music for a while that we were missing the point of the whole thing. We had become lethargic and realised that we were relying on the music to take us into a place of supernatural fireworks. We had missed that heart of worship: relationship with Jesus. To try and sort it out we banned the music and the musicians, sat on the floor and if someone wanted to start up a song they did. We all had to ask what the sacrifice of praise was that *we* were bringing, how hungry we were to pursue our own relationship with God. We had to learn, through a bit of pain, that no matter what the setting, worship is about me and Jesus, and that . . .

> when the music fades and all is stripped away, and I simply come, longing just to bring something that's of worth, that will bless your heart, I'll bring you more than a song. For a song in itself is not what you have required: you search much deeper within than the way things appear, you're looking into my heart. I'm coming back to the heart of worship and it's all about you, Jesus.

For us as a church this became the most profound song that we knew. It reminded, encouraged and warned us about the core of our relationship with God. Again we knew that worship is not self-indulgence, but giving our hearts to him.

The job of the worship leader is to lead the people into God's presence so that they can give him his worth-ship (which is kind of like a ship, but full of all the good things that God deserves). The job of the worship leader is always to draw attention to Jesus, and never to draw attention to themselves by performing.

There was a donkey who returned home one day particularly flushed with excitement (I say 'particularly' as

he had always been a fairly excitable donkey). 'Mum,' he said, 'you'll never guess what happened to me today. It was fantastic; I was just minding my own business being tied to a gatepost and these two men came and got me. They led me down the street and everyone came out of their houses and they were all cheering me and clapping and they were putting their cloaks in front of me, and they were tearing the branches off the trees and waving them at me and putting them on the floor in front of me. Mum,' (big pause) 'I was famous! They did all this for your little donkey son, Mum – it was wonderful.'

'Oh, my little donkey boy,' replied his mum, when he had calmed down a little, 'when they were clapping and cheering and throwing the branches in front, they weren't doing it for you. They were doing it for the one you were carrying.'

At the risk of sounding like a nagging parent myself, that's exactly what I keep on saying to our worship leaders: 'Remember, you are only the donkey, it's the one you're carrying who is important.'

The whole picture

Getting back to the wider concept of worship, it seems to me that worship through music is the activity of the Church gathered, while worship as a way of life is the activity of the Church scattered. The Church needs to be active when it is meeting together, just as it needs to be active during the other six days of the week. If we favour one over another we lose the balance that's so crucial to our faith. The words without the actions are worse than irrelevant; they are actively despised by God. Equally, the works without the communication don't make for a relationship with God.

This is not to say that we Christians have the monopoly on Good Works – I don't believe that someone of another (or no) faith can't bring justice into the world. To the homeless person, perhaps a roof over their head is the same whether it comes via an atheist or a Christian. The difference is that we *have to* go and work among the 'poor' – it's part of the deal. When we serve the poor, when we do good, we do it for God, drawing closer to him and further away from our comforts.

As we try to fulfil our part of the bargain in this way, doing it for his sake, we tune in to his compassion. Our own compassion can become tired and even distorted, but at least with God we have a chance to continually return to the source of all compassion, the source of all goodness.

John chapter 12 contains the most profound description of worship that I know. As Martha busied herself with the arrangements, Mary Magdalene poured the litre jar full of perfume over Jesus' feet, wiping them with her hair. The perfume itself was worth over a year's wages and offended Judas, who was the light-fingered keeper of the money. He complained about the waste, about the fact that at his feet was a puddle of smelly liquid worth over eighteen grand – and he was right. It was the most extravagant act of adoration, and it remains the best model of worship that we can find. Worship is wasting ourselves on God. It may start with singing a song, but before long it invades our money, our time, our talents and the rest of our lives. The key to the story comes at the end of verse 3, which says that 'the house was filled with the fragrance of the perfume'. When we truly waste ourselves on Jesus, whether it is with others, whether it is by spending time with him on our own, or whether it is by caring for the poor, something invisible and indescribable will fill the air, something wonderful will happen.

> True worship is to be so personally and hopelessly in love with God that the idea of a transfer of affection never even remotely exists.
>
> (A.W. Tozer)

Live it!

'. . . To be so personally and hopelessly in love with God that the idea of a transfer of affection never even remotely exists.' Wow. I mean, just how HUGE does that sound? Of course it sounds wonderful, right? After all, to be so caught up in God, to be so head over heals and fully fired up to do anything for him, well, that's bound to have a few knock on effects isn't it? I mean, can you imagine if a whole nation were like that? Can you imagine what life would be like if people were all pulling in the same direction, all aiming to serve God with all their might, all desperate to put him first and themselves second? It would be different, to say the least.

But does this really help us? Does it make sense getting caught up in some fantasy about how life would be so much better *if only there were more of us*? Worship, you see, is not about making life easier for us. Worship is about doing what is right, about an attempt to give God more and more of what he deserves. Worship is not about us: it's about him. Yes the world would be a very different place if you added a few zeros onto the numbers of God's worshippers, but let's not buy into the idea that our worship would be worth more if only there were more of us. God is not obsessed with size, and biggest is not always best. Your worship, your life lived with radical passion and true commitment to him, is worth it. It's what he deserves. Let's not dream of tomorrow while we let ourselves off the hook for today: let's be serious about what God deserves from each of us.

Task

Think of as many ways as possible of showing God that someone could be 'personally and hopelessly in love' with him. Look back over some of the passages mentioned in this chapter: John 12, Matthew 25, Psalm 22. Does reading these help you add any more expressions of worship to your list?

Worship of God is about the whole life, about living it out loud for him through sacrifice, risk, generosity, humility and integrity. It is also about drawing close to God, about adoration, about *proskuneo*. Take time to draw these two threads together, to draw close to God in intimacy and tenderness. Offer yourself as a sacrifice to him, take on the role of the donkey so that the kingdom of God might spread even further around you.

3

Tea, toast and tortoises

(a chapter about prayer)

Face facts, we're not very good at prayer. Sin, now that's a different story, we seem to be doing fairly well there, but prayer – well, ever since the disciples slumbered in the garden of Gethsemane it seems like it's got us well and truly beaten. Or has it? Lately God has been rousing the Church with a desire to tune into the things that set his heart on fire and pray accordingly. Strip away the kneeling and the olde English language and prayer is basically communication with God. There are many types of prayer: confession, adoration, thanksgiving. In this chapter we are going to look at one aspect of prayer – asking. This is known in the trade as intercession, and it's a world away from my early attempts at prayer, which always ended up with me dribbling on to my sleeve as I fell into a deep, deep sleep.

But whatever the style of prayer we're focusing on, we Christians find it one of the easiest things to get on a guilt trip about. How many times have we bought the line, 'God couldn't use you, you don't pray enough'? Like all good lies it's based on a little truth: after all, how much is enough? Two hours out of twenty-four doesn't sound like much at all – but the thought of a four-hour quiet time would send most of us into a deep panic. The truth is that we need to learn to relax a little and know that life can be a prayer, and learn to spend time communicating with our Father in heaven. However, while it's possible to communicate with someone you love without saying anything, there comes a time when there's nothing for it but to have a good chat. Instead of making prayer and intercession a legalistic 'you ought to say your prayers, you ought to have your quiet time', it's helpful to get back to basics and find out exactly what it is that drives us to pray.

Four steps to a sorted prayer life

One day Jesus was praying in a certain place. When he finished, one of his disciples said to him, 'Lord, teach us to pray, just as John taught his disciples.' He said to them, 'When you pray, say:

"Father, hallowed be your name, your kingdom come. Give us each day our daily bread. Forgive us our sins, for we also forgive everyone who sins against us. And lead us not into temptation." '

Then he said to them, 'Suppose one of you has a friend and he goes to him at midnight and says, "Friend, lend me three loaves of bread, because a friend of mine on a journey has come to me, and I have nothing to set before him." Then the one inside answers, "Don't bother me. The door is already locked, and my children are with me in bed. I can't get up and give you anything." I tell you, though he will not get up and give him the bread because he is his friend, yet because of the man's boldness he will get up and give him as much as he needs.

'So I say to you: Ask and it will be given to you; seek and you will find; knock and the door will be opened to you. For everyone who asks receives; he who seeks finds; and to him who knocks, the door will be opened.'

(Luke 11:1–10)

1 The need

Like in every good detective novel, the clues are scattered all around the Bible. In the text quoted above Jesus does some major hint-dropping. The scenario of an out-of-town friend turning up shows four conditions for prayer, without which it is dull and lifeless. The visitor is in desperate need of a bit of tea and toast, so desperate that he wakes up his friend in the middle of the night. I wouldn't get up for anyone in the middle of the night unless it was really, really important and I loved them more than I love my bed (which is a lot). And so the host fulfils the first condition for prayer: he has a need.

2 Nothing to give

The cupboard is bare; there's no sign of the necessary Mighty White and Tetley. Realising that he can't come up with the goods himself, he knows that he needs help from somewhere else. In order to get prayer sorted, we need to realise that our own intelligence, money, popularity and resources cannot meet the needs of the world, or the specific needs of those around us.

3 I know a God who can

The host knows that his neighbour has plenty of the necessary. Do we believe that God has exactly what we need? If we do we'll get on our knees, just as the man went to his neighbour's door and we'll . . .

4 Keep on asking

Verses 7 and 8 of our passage from Luke refer to the toast-hunter's boldness being the deciding factor in getting the neighbour out of bed. The footnote that accompanies the verses suggests that the word 'boldness' could also be described as 'persistence'. The original Greek takes it even further, implying that the man was being so bold as to be almost cheeky. However, when we start praying it some-times feels as if God's tucked up in his bed and can't be bothered to answer. At those times we give up, thinking that it would be rude to keep on asking, but it's at those times more than any other that we need to do as we're told and keep on knocking on the door, determined to wake up the whole neighbourhood if necessary.

Of course, none of this means that we should think of God as a glorified caterer, turning up whenever we click our fingers. We need to believe that God wants us to pray; we need to understand that God wants us to feel about things as passionately as he does.

God speed

This brings us into a head-on conflict between the way that we like things to happen and the way that they actually do. We love the lightning-quick answers to prayer. Occasionally they do happen, but for most of the time they are a little on the rare side, leaving us frustrated and offended at God's apparent lack of interest. The truth, according to Colin Urquhart, is that the Lord often answers in two ways: with the Lightning Response and with the Tortoise Response. The Lightning Response is exciting and immediate, but more often the Lord sends down his messenger complete with answer in shell – the Tortoise Response. Often the little fellow has only managed to get halfway before we've got bored and have given up all hope of ever receiving an answer. Knowing that we've given up, the tortoise turns round and goes home. While I'm not sure exactly how far we can take this picture (if God uses tortoises, what happens when they hibernate?), I reckon it's a pretty good bit of encouragement to persevere in prayer.

I have posted watchmen on your walls, O Jerusalem; they will never be silent day or night,

You who call on the Lord give yourselves no rest,
  and give him no rest till he establishes Jerusalem
and makes her the praise of the earth.

(Isa. 62:6–7)

Here is another instruction from God to be cheeky in prayer.
He says that we must never give up until he answers.

Sauce!

Another example of biblical cheek is when God slips
Abraham his plans for a reshuffle of Sodom, a city that was
constantly topping the Most Unrighteous City charts.
Abraham's response is simple but effective; he tries to blag
it. Displaying bartering skills that any second-hand car
dealer would be proud of, he manages to knock God down
from saving the city for a hundred righteous people to a
mere ten. Through his reverent cheek Abraham manages
to influence God.

But does this mean that, left on his own, God would be
making poor decisions? Do we have to watch his every
move like a warden in a retirement home in case he sets fire
to his dressing gown? Of course not. The truth is that God
loves it when we get our prayer-fangs stuck into something
because it means that we are developing our relationship
with him.

Surprise!

This also provides the answer to one of those questions
that always used to trip me up: what's the point in continually asking God to do something that he wants to do
anyway? When we're interceding God often does more than
just answer our prayers: in getting closer to him we can't
fail to be changed. Put another way, the tortoise often has a
few surprises tucked up his shell.

In Ezekiel chapter 4 we see that the prophet was on the

receiving end of one or two of those surprises. There are certain passages of Scripture that you can become so familiar with that you actually forget what they are about. For me the book of Ezekiel, the story of one of God's nuttiest prophets, is precisely one of those passages. As well as showing God's love for his people, it makes a potent statement about the value of intercession, and shows Ezekiel going through all sorts of pain but ending up infinitely closer to God.

Ezekiel is told by God to 'take a clay tablet, put it in front of you and draw the city of Jerusalem on it'. His next instruction is to 'lay siege to it', to bring on his pretend soldiers and have himself a little war game. Rather strange perhaps, but in the privacy of your own home this might not be too worrying. The trouble was that God wanted this particular display of prophetic Lego to be a very public one.

As Ezekiel lay on his left side he was giving the whole of Israel a sign: not of his flimsy grip on reality, but of their firm grasp of disobedience. For 390 days Ezekiel lay on his side, each day symbolising a year of Israel's sin. He then lay on his right side for forty days, when each day represented a year of the sin of the house of Judah. For over fourteen months he lay in front of his reconstruction of Israel, tied up with ropes and eating no more than 200 grams of unleavened bread per day. At the end of it all God told him to stand up and, 'with bared arm', prophesy to Israel. His naked arm wouldn't have been a pretty sight after a year of being squashed by Ezekiel's body (can you imagine the bedsores?).

As he lifted his arm to speak to Israel he would have felt something of the pain that God would have felt for the 390 years of Israel's sin. Ezekiel's physical and mental state would have meant that his words would not have been packaged with the polite niceties we often hear today ('Excuse me, Israel, but you've been a bit naughty now, haven't you?' would not have been his opening phrase). As he spat out the words he felt the absolute pain of the torture he had endured, and touched a part of God's heart that had suffered the same. Ezekiel's story gives us a clear job description for the prophetic intercessor: it is to feel God's pain. That's why we often end up weeping when we pray.

The Christmas List Crisis

As a slightly younger human being I suffered a yearly dose of anxiety each time the Christmas decorations went up. Should I make a present list or go for the surprises? A list, you may think, would be the obvious choice, but being a particularly innocent young pup I was especially vulnerable when it came to the latest Big Thing. Whatever I was willing to lose a limb for in November I would be desperately

trying to dismantle in December. I spent many a Christmas Day devising devious plans to sell on my brand new boxed item in order to upgrade it to the vastly superior version that I had seen only the day before. My parents' choices were little better, and if I'd taken the option marked 'Surprise' every year I would have ended up with enough junior chemistry sets to run a hospital. Things are a little calmer now, but every once in a while I go through a similar crisis about prayer. Are my constant requests to God any better than my childhood desire for the newest, biggest and best? After all, just what should we be praying for? Is it even right to keep on asking God for all these things?

Back to basics: God likes us to pray and to believe that he will answer. In one conversation Jesus says:

And I will do whatever you ask in my name, so that the Son may bring glory to the Father. You may ask me for anything in my name, and I will do it.

(John 14:13–14)

If you remain in me and my words remain in you, ask whatever you wish, and it will be given you.

(John 15:7)

You did not choose me, but I chose you and appointed you to go and bear fruit – fruit that will last. Then the Father will give you whatever you ask in my name.

(John 15:16)

Until now you have not asked for anything in my name. Ask and you will receive, and your joy will be complete.

(John 16:24)

Do you think Jesus was trying to tell them something?

Unfortunately this doesn't quite give us a blank cheque with which to go out and bag a Porsche or win the Lottery, so what are the boundaries? John 15:7 gives us the clue. 'If you remain in me and my words remain in you, ask whatever you wish and it will be given you.' That seems to me a good verse for intercessors. Spending time with God, remaining in him, depending on him like a branch on a vine, will get us closer to him and closer to his heart. The closer we are to his heart, the more likely we are to be in tune with what God wants. Avoiding the Christmas List Crisis, spending time with God is a sure way to be asking for the right things.

So I have to give up what I'm doing now and lie on my side for the next year, do I?

Good point. Most of us would find it hard to be a full-time player in the Ezekiel league of prophetic intercession, but does that mean that our prayer lives are non-starters? Certainly not, for though there will be some who are made for that side of things, to whom, perhaps, those stories really speak, most of us will find a slightly less intense rhythm of prayer. Returning to the start of the chapter, prayer starts when we see a need, realise that we can't sort it ourselves and believe that God can help. This applies to both the fall of a nation and the pain of a friend. God cares about both and hears the prayers with equal compassion.

But what if we lack the time or the energy to intercede for hours on end? Is it an all-or-nothing situation, where if we don't lock ourselves away for twelve hours a day we might as well not bother at all? I hope not. Perhaps we see prayer in too narrow terms. I think there is a place for knuckling down and concentrating on speaking to the Lord, but equally valid is spending time chatting with him.

There's a place for taking a walk, talking to the Lord with the backdrop of his creation.

Often I'll pray in tongues in all sorts of locations, and I believe that's a powerful way of working out with God. I remember when I first heard of this bizarre, magical gift that only a select few ever received. I thought that speaking in tongues was like a knighthood: only given if you were part of the in-crowd, but pretty useless when you'd got it. Still, I fancied getting me some, so I asked a couple of friends in the church to give it to me. They soon put me straight, suggesting that we ask God to give it to me instead. The plan was pretty simple (almost too simple, I thought, but I didn't want to burst their bubble); we would ask God to give me the gift of tongues, then they would start to speak in tongues themselves. After a while one of them would touch my lips and I would say the first thing that came to my mouth.

I began to get nervous once we reached the lip-touching stage. Until then I had simply been enjoying the beautiful sound of their strange language, but now I realised that I would have to pull something pretty impressive out of the bag if I wasn't going to disappoint. I had my hands out-stretched and my eyes shut, but I could feel them willing me on. There was no point in delaying so I went for it.

'SHALLA BALLA.' I stood up to get my coat.

'Oh, thank you, Lord,' said one of them.

'Yes, thank you for giving Mike the gift of tongues,' said the other.

They both wore smiles that matched their words and seemed genuinely convinced that I was the recipient of a genuine Spiritual Gift and not a Verbal Breakdown. I had another go.

'SHALLA BALLA, BEELA BALLA.'

This made them even more excited, so I pitched in with a few more words.

After an hour we stopped and had a chat. They understood my surprise that it all seemed so simple, and told me that it was just about another way of praying when we don't quite know what to pray. They suggested that I spent ten minutes doing it each day, learning to communicate with God. It made such a difference to our relationship that I've stuck with it ever since.

In the New Testament we see many people speaking in tongues, using it as a prayer language. There are many times when we are stuck for knowing how or what to pray, or even how to express our love for God. The gift of tongues is the Holy Spirit praying within us. When we start it can sound like baby-talk, as it did with me, but I eventually found out that the secret is not to concentrate on what is being said, but to focus on Jesus. I have found it to be one of the biggest helps imaginable in my prayer life.

Another way is to pray the Scriptures; why not take a psalm or one of the great prayers of the Bible and read them out as your prayer to God? Thankfully we are all different, and what might be helpful for one person may be a waste of time for another. The important thing to remember is that we all need to find the ways of praying that work for us. Whatever the situation, it is always possible to pause and take a little time out with God, which, after all, is a pretty good way of getting closer to him and understanding what he wants for our lives.

Live it!

What is prayer all about? Can we twist God's arm? Does God act as a democracy, only rousing from his slumber when a certain number of prayer-votes have been cast? Thankfully the answer is a definite 'no', but there are plenty of reasons still kicking around for us to get down on our knees and take our requests to our heavenly Father.

Remember that quote from John 15:7, the one where the writer points out that 'If you remain in me and my words remain in you, ask whatever you wish, and it will be given you' – it strikes me that this gets right to the heart of the matter. Yeah, there's that tempting line about how whatever we wish will be given to us, but it's a line that cannot be taken solo: it has to be accompanied by the urge that we get as close to God as possible. And there we have it: intercession is as much about establishing and developing our relationship with God as it is about unpacking the spiritual presents that get sent down from on high. In other words, it's less about what we get and more about what we can give.

Let's face it, this is bad news for anyone who suffers like I do from the temptation to opt for the easy path of Christianity. I'm embarrassed to admit it, but too often I see prayer as a badge that proves I'm spiritually on track rather than a tool for getting closer to God. In other words when I sit down to pray I'm telling God that this is my way of showing what a good Christian I'm being: 'Look God,' I say, 'I'm asking you to do all these things so surely that means I'm doing well, doesn't it?' Occasionally – and I do mean occasionally – things go slightly better and intercession becomes a blank canvas, an opportunity for me to try to hear what God might be saying about what's on his heart. I like those times the best.

Task

Why did Ezekiel lay on his side for so long?

    a for publicity
    b because he got cramp
    c because God told him to

You get the picture.

Find some time to pray – but not just alone in your room with heavy eyelids. Try experimenting with different environments: walking, running or sitting; indoors or outdoors; creating something with your hands or contemplating an object like a cross or a candle. What should you pray about? Ask God to show you. Simple as that.

4

God whispers to his friends

(a chapter about listening to God)

Hear the word 'prophecy' and what do you think? Strange people with big hair and peculiar diets? Messages that start out 'I have a picture of a sheep . . .'? The truth is that prophecy is one of the aspects of the Christian life we seem to misunderstand and even forget about altogether. Whether we leave it because we think it's mystical or dismiss it as mundane, we run the risk of missing out on hearing God's voice, receiving his direction and fuelling up on his power. To take it back to basics, we believe in a God who speaks. He has always been speaking to his people, and he speaks to us today. For many of us the biggest problem is knowing how to hear him, knowing how to recognise his voice – and boy, do we need to hear the voice of God today.

I used to think that prophecy was limited to certain meetings. You know the ones: a circle of chairs in the church hall where, after a while, someone gets up and says, 'I have a picture of a waterfall/lake/river . . .' There's nothing wrong with this, but it wasn't until a few years ago that I realised that biblical prophecy, the sort we see throughout the Scriptures, is totally relevant to every aspect of our lives today. It's about God talking to us. It's about the Church becoming people led not by good ideas but by his voice and Spirit.

Doing my bit for the European Union

A while back I spent three years as youth worker at St Andrew's Chorleywood. When I finished, my boss, Bishop David Pytches, found me another job in the church, and I didn't think twice about it until the day came when I actually stopped being the youth worker and HE started. With his arrival came the thought, 'What have I done? They're *my* young people, they belong to me and he's got them.' I remember the first Friday they met with him: I sat in my flat, praying and trying to be holy, asking the Lord to bless my (ex) youth group with their new leader. I cancelled the prayers pretty quickly. The whole thing hurt, and to my surprise I went through a real bereavement process. For the next six months I grieved and missed them terribly, all of which was made worse by the fact that I didn't feel settled or fulfilled in the new job. I started to think about leaving.

Then I went to France with a friend who also worked at the church. Barry and I were going to run a youth conference, and as we were driving I told Barry how I was feeling. When we arrived we met up with the local pastors to have a meal and talk about the conference. We hadn't met before so they knew nothing about me. At the end of the meal we decided to pray, and in the middle of the prayer time one of the pastors got up and walked away from the table. He went to the coat stand and picked up a little girl's duffelcoat, then walked back and stood in front of me. Holding the coat open, he spoke.

'Poot zuh cout on!' he said.

'Oh dear,' I thought. I shrugged a silent reply that said, 'I can't,' and hoped that he might go and ask someone else to join in his little game.

'Poot zuh cout on!' he repeated.

'I can't,' I said. Desperately in need of support I looked at Barry, who looked down and closed his eyes. Again the

demented pastor with poor vision asked me to put it on. In the hope of avoiding an international incident I tried to put my fingers in the sleeve.

'I can't,' I said as I tried to get my hand out again.

'Why not?'

Now I knew what I was dealing with. Slowly, pronouncing every syllable as if my entire reputation depended upon it, I replied, 'BECAUSE IT DOES NOT FIT.'

'Exactly,' came the reply, 'and God says to you, "Stop running back and trying to put on the old coat. It doesn't fit you any more." Let God give you the new coat, the new ministry. You're feeling naked because you're between ministries. Don't run back to the thing that's safe, let God give you the new coat. Put the new ministry on.'

Suddenly I was shaken by the realisation that God really does exist – and he knows about me. It didn't make everything perfect but I knew that God knew me and that he had a plan for me. It was so right for me at the time, and I had never encountered anything like it before. This guy was willing to take a risk and God spoke profoundly through it, just as we see in Scripture.

Hungry for more

I returned home desperate to hear God speak as powerfully as the French pastor, but didn't know how. I started reading passages of Scripture in a new way; in 1 Corinthians 14:1 it says, 'Follow the way of love and eagerly desire the spiritual gifts, especially the gift of prophecy.' That means that we are to be keen to get our hands on those spiritual gifts like nothing else. Until the penny dropped I had been pretty cool about them. 'O Lord,' I had prayed, 'I will not seek after the gifts, I am simply happy with the Giver.' I thought I was being spiritual and holy, but it was a pretty false and unbiblical spirituality. In not wanting to be a 'gift junky' and ignoring God's gifts, I was ignoring God, missing out on the chance to get a lot closer to him. Reading what Paul wrote to the church at Corinth it is clear that 'eagerly desiring . . . especially the gift of prophecy' is not about being self-indulgent, but leads directly to our being strengthened, encouraged and comforted (1 Cor. 14:3). This is the purpose of New Testament prophecy.

Prophecy is not meant to be a substitute for the word of God: we must never lose the study of the Book in favour of the Lord giving us a quick prophecy instead of a quiet time. Reading the Bible is by far the best way to hear God and to learn more about his character. Maybe we don't see so much of God waving Mothercare duffelcoats around in the Bible, but we do see him giving encouragement and guidance to his children. Throughout the book of Acts there are loads of instances where the Apostles recognised God's voice and put his commands into action as they established the early Church. Prophecy is as relevant today as it was then.

For a while after I returned from France I was asking the Lord to teach me about hearing him speak, when I met a vicar called Bruce Collins. We were both involved in a retreat for church leaders run by St Andrew's, and every six weeks or so, on the last night of each course, Bruce would come and pray for each person and ask God to speak. I heard about this and I asked if I could go along. Everyone took it in turns to be prayed for by Bruce and a member of his team while all the others sat around and prayed. I found it hard to believe what I saw and heard, as each time Bruce or someone from his team would speak prophetic words that were incredibly accurate and helpful. Everybody seemed to be strengthened and encouraged and comforted when God spoke. I knew that I was seeing people's lives being changed for good, right in front of me.

I ran through a little check-list in my head to see if I thought the words were from God. Did what was said line up with the Scriptures? Were the people left strengthened, encouraged and comforted as a result? Did it lead people to Jesus? When the Lord spoke to me in France, my response wasn't, 'Oh, isn't this French pastor wonderful,' but it was to worship Jesus. Revelation chapter 19 verse 10 says that 'the Testimony of Jesus is the spirit of prophecy'.

At the end of the first meeting I went up to Bruce and told him how much I wanted to be able to hear God. I think I was feeling a bit annoyed because I'd tried so hard since I returned from France to get the gift of prophecy, but all I had managed to get was the gift of frustration. I'd tried so hard to tune in and Be Prophetic but all that I came up with was the word 'spaghetti'. There's nothing wrong with the word, but there's only so much you can do with it: 'You're worried about your job? God says that it is like spaghetti: you've got too much on your plate,' or 'You think you might be pregnant? God says spaghetti: it's quite good for you.' I told Bruce about this and he said I needed to practise listening to God, and that I could come along to help at the next Prophecy Night.

Embarrassment

Because it was six weeks away I agreed to do it. I had originally intended to pray and fast until the meeting so that I might be spiritually prepared, but it didn't seem to happen. I completely forgot until the day came when I was supposed to sit next to Bruce and prophesy to these sixteen church leaders and their spouses. When I realised, that afternoon, I prayed that I would be sick, I prayed that they would be sick, I prayed for the Second Coming. At 7.30 p.m. I went along and I sat next to Bruce while he explained a little bit about how God speaks. I was working on Plan B, getting my reserve words ready ('The Lord says, "You're a woman"') but I knew I'd get caught out so I began to bargain: 'Please, Lord, give me a prophecy, just this once. I'll pray every day for the rest of my life. I'll be a missionary.'

The first couple came forward and we started to pray. By this time I was getting frantic, hearing a mixture of silence and total internal panic. But then, ever so faintly I began to hear a song. Could this be a prophetic song, speaking truth and power in a beautiful tongue? I strained to work out what it was, getting ready to deliver, and then it hit me. Abba, 'Dancing Queen'.

'Leave it out, Lord, give me something sensible,' was my most spiritual reaction. Bruce had pretty much finished giving his words, and I knew I didn't have much time. He (along with everyone else) turned to me.

'And Mike, what do you have?'

I smiled, closed my eyes and prayed: 'Lord, you've got five seconds.' When it was clear that there was nothing other than the Swedish pop combo's Greatest Dance Hall Classic in my head, I knew I had to say it. I took a good look at this vicar's wife and got ready to throw my entire (but small) reputation out the window.

'I think the Lord would say to you, in the words of Abba, "You can dance, you can jive, having the time of your life." ' And then I wanted to die.

The lady started to laugh. 'Cheers,' I thought. 'If ever I meet you and you make a fool of yourself I hope I'm there to have a good giggle too.'

'I suppose you're wondering why we're laughing,' she said when she had calmed down a little.

'No,' I thought.

'Three weeks ago, I started a dance group in my church with two other women. As we were coming to this meeting, I said to my husband – didn't I, dear – what am I doing starting a dance group? I shouldn't be doing something like that, I can't dance.'

Verses 6 to 8 of Numbers chapter 12 seem to explain the whole Abba thing. Aaron and Miriam were complaining to God about Moses when they were given this reply.

When a prophet of the LORD is among you,
    I reveal myself to him in visions,
    I speak to him in dreams.
But this is not true of my servant Moses;
    He is faithful in all my house.
With him I speak face to face,
    clearly and not in riddles;
    he sees the form of the LORD.
Why then were you not afraid
    to speak against my servant Moses?

If you think about it, God says that, apart from Moses, he speaks to the rest of his prophets in visions, dreams, and riddles. He doesn't speak clearly. That means that spending a life listening to God speak could very well include a whole load more Abba incidents. Great!

God whispers to his friends

So why does God speak like that? Besides the obvious benefit of keeping people like me firmly in their place, one reason, I suspect, is to stretch our faith. The Scripture says that 'we prophesy according to our faith'. If God spoke to us prophetically by going, 'Hear ye, hear ye, God calling. Mike, are you receiving me?' there would be little place for faith, for taking a risk and choosing to believe in God. Perhaps another reason is that God is more interested in relationship with us than in anything else. It's fair to say from Scripture that God shouts to his enemies and whispers to his friends. Jesus said to his disciples, 'You are my friends. I reveal the secrets of heaven to you, my friends.' He revealed those secrets with whispering parables, examples and actions, things that started the disciples thinking, things that drew them close to him.

I was at my sister's house a few years ago when my six-year-old niece walked into the room. 'Jo, come here.

Mummy wants to tell you something,' said my sister, and Jo, being six, said, 'NO.'

'Come here, Mummy's got a secret to tell you.'

'What's the secret?' said Jo.

'If Mummy told you from here to there, it wouldn't be a secret because everyone else in the room would hear.'

Getting a little excited, Jo said, 'Tell me now,' and moved a few paces closer.

'The secret's this . . .'

'What?' Jo said.

'You'll have to come closer.' Jo came closer – and it was too late. My sister grabbed hold of her and said, 'The secret's this – Mummy loves you!' and kissed her.

Afterwards I thought that sometimes God whispers to us to make us get so close that we really listen to him. No one has a special hotline to God, it's just a matter of responding to him when he asks us to get closer. I used to repent before I saw Bruce; I thought that if he looked into my eyes he would see all my sin. Thankfully that's not the way it works; God wants us to get closer to him so that we can be strengthened, encouraged and comforted, not so that we can get the dirt on our mates.

More embarrassments

Later that year we were having another prophecy meeting with the visiting clergy. I remember meeting one couple. The wife said to me, 'Hello, you're Greek aren't you?' I said I was and she told me that she had lived in Athens for a while. Before she had a chance to ask me if I knew a guy with a moustache called Costas, the meeting started.

As we were praying for her this Greek swear word came into my mind. Trying not to look embarrassed I started thinking about something else, but it was no good. The word was *skadula* which means 'female excrement'. Then as we were praying I thought, 'What's the point? If she doesn't know the word it won't mean anything and if she does she'll smack me!'

Bruce then chipped in. 'Mike, I think God's given you something.'

I tried to use some common sense, so phrasing my question carefully I asked her, 'When you lived in Greece, did people say bad words to you?'

Straight away tears came into her eyes and she said, 'Yes.'

I said, 'The Lord wants to say to you that in his eyes you are not a skadula.'

I couldn't believe the response. She sobbed and sobbed. She had lived in Greece and married a Greek man who abused her, giving her the nickname Skadula. He used to introduce her to his friends as 'my Skadula'. God broke through and started to heal her in an amazing way. That's how it works.

There are plenty of people who could tell a lot better stories of how God has worked in the prophetic, and it's important to remember that this gift is for all of us. We need to eagerly desire the spiritual gifts, especially prophecy, and we need to take the word seriously. As we do it he will speak to us and in faith we will begin to speak words. Sometimes we will get it wrong. This is the way we learn to tell what comes from God and what comes from our own imagination.

And another embarrassment

Even though I would much rather you get it wrong for yourselves, I suppose I'd better let you know about one of my best/worst times ever. When I was beginning to learn about prophecy I went to the Isle of Man to speak at some meetings. In the first one we prayed for some words, and got some that seemed to be fairly accurate. The congregation had never experienced it before, and they seemed very encouraged by it. So we kept on and spent quite a bit of time on it during the week, during which God was really good to all of us.

Before the final meeting, where about three hundred people came from different parts of the island, I was sitting on the toilet minding my own business. A couple of guys were outside my cubicle, unaware of the fact that I was in there. One guy said to the other, 'Oh, I can't wait for tonight. That Mike Pilavachi is so amazing, such a prophet. God's going to give him some awesome words tonight.' I sat there with a satisfied smile on my face and told the Lord that we were going to do a great meeting.

After the worship I strode on, accompanied by my Prophetic Look. I spent a few minutes strolling up and down, staring at people and twitching my eyebrows. I looked good! Suddenly I stopped when I saw a woman and the phrase 'Put on your dancing shoes' came into my mind. It seemed to be a good one so I gave it a go.

'That lady there, would you stand? God is about to speak to you!' I announced in my deepest, most prophetic voice. 'The Lord would say unto you, "Put on your dancing shoes." ' I looked around as everyone was waiting in rapt attention. 'Would you like to share how you've been blessed by that word?'

She stood there in silence for some time, looking a bit awkward. I decided to help her with the interpretation.

'Do you dance?'

'Not really,' she said.

'Aah! You don't dance!' I replied, confident that this would be the launch of one of the most powerful dancing careers of the century.

'Yes, I do sometimes, alone in the room. Not too much, not too little.'

I tried hard to find a spiritual significance, and I remembered that passage from Psalm 30 that says 'He turned my wailing into dancing.' I decided this must be it. 'Perhaps you're in mourning? Has someone close to you died?'

She paused. 'I don't think so. A woman down the road died six months ago, but I hardly knew her.'

There followed one of the most embarrassing moments of my life as this woman and I tried every way to make the word fit. Eventually I realised what was going on, and I had to face up and say to everyone, 'Sorry, folks, I got that one wrong.' I've had a lot of 'good' times like that.

If you are looking for a reason why that happens, the answer is one of the clearest that you can find in Scripture. There's a passage that's repeated three times, which is very rare for the Bible. The verse can be found in Proverbs, in the book of James and in the first letter of Peter: 'God opposes the proud and gives grace to the humble.' God repeats it because he means it. Since that's the truth, I vote for humbling myself from now on – it's a lot less painful. We will get it wrong, so let's not pretend. Anyway, prophecy is more about us getting closer to God than it is about us climbing higher than our friends.

Often we don't expect to hear, so we don't listen or jot things down. Put this book down and begin to listen to the Lord. You don't need to go up to people and say, 'The Lord told me,' 'The Lord says' or 'I know your secret sin.' Sometimes offering to pray for the person next to you in church is the best way to say what you believe God is saying to you. We will all fail as we develop the gift of prophecy, but as we do let's keep in mind the basic truth; let's not super-spiritualise things. God whispers to us, his friends, not because he fancies a laugh or wants to make us look good, but because he loves us and wants us close to him.

Live it!

Embarrassment after embarrassment; I just can't seem to separate examples of hearing God speak from situations where I've come across like a fool. But while it might dent my ego a bit, deep down I know that this is the right way round: to try to rely on God to do the miracles instead of ourselves. And perhaps this is something that can help us live the life, as too often we get caught up in the trap that says that prophecy only really works when used in church services. After all, many of us see it used most often at the end of the meeting, so why shouldn't we assume that it is at those times that God whispers the most. While this might be nice and cosy, unfortunately it's also wrong. God's whispers are not secret code delivered just to keep us Christians amused while we're on the journey: they're the very breath of God.

Task

The book of Acts is packed full of details of how the early Christians went about living the life to full effect. It might take you a while, but look through the book for any examples you can find of the key players using prophecy as they went about their lives. Start in chapter three if you like, where Peter and John meet up with the beggar outside the temple gate.

What do these examples tell you about how and why God whispers to his friends? Can you think of ways in which God's whispers might have an impact on the lives of people around you as you go about your day?

What next? Practise listening and passing the whispers on.

Part II
Getting Steady

5

The yeast in your beer

(this one's about faith)

Faith – you can lose it, gain it, share it and heal with it. To some people just having it will sort you out when your body is six feet under; to others it's enough to kill for. Some talk of good and bad faith; others talk listlessly of not having it, as if it were similar to a heated towel rail. Face facts: it's confusing, and with so many opinions going round it can be kind of hard to sort out. Starting at first base, then . . .

What is faith?

Whatever it is, the Bible is full of it. More than that, it seems that Jesus got really excited about it too. For example, when the centurion said to Jesus, 'You don't need to come to my house to heal my servant, I'm a man under authority, all you have to do is say the word,' Jesus came out with a five-star endorsement. 'I've not seen so much faith in the whole of Israel,' he said. At other times Jesus healed the sick and added, 'because of your faith you've been made well'. He loved to see faith in people.

God not only loves faith, it also brings him pleasure. Hebrews chapter 11 verse 6 pulls no punches with the line, 'And without faith it is impossible to please God.' Anyone who comes to God must believe that he exists and that he rewards those who earnestly seek him. That's potentially a fairly depressing thought, and I have heard more than a few people say, 'I wish I could believe, but I just don't have the faith.' To many, faith is an unscalable object that's best left alone. Thankfully that doesn't have to be the case, and God loves to tickle our hearts and get us interested. Sooner or later, it's time to sign on the dotted line.

Is faith something that you think?
To an extent, yes. Our Christian faith is based on concrete evidence. Part of the success of the Alpha course has come from its commitment to exploring the facts of Christianity (how do we know Christ lived? how do we know that it's real?). Knowing the facts of Christianity is vital to faith, especially at times when nothing feels right.

Is faith something that you feel?
This is right too. There may have been times in your life when you have known that God is real, when it all seems to make sense and life is great. Chances are, if you've experienced this then you've touched the other side of the coin: nothing is real, nothing works and nothing exists. Feelings are unfortunately unreliable, but shouldn't be sniffed at. The times when you sincerely believe that God is going to do something are great, but can't be relied upon to be there every time we call on him. The sort of faith that we see throughout the Bible is a little more than something that you think or feel. One of the biggest clues available can be found in Mark 2.

A few days later, when Jesus again entered Capernaum, the people heard that he had come home. So many gathered that there was no room left, not even outside the door, and he preached the word to them. Some men came, bringing to him a paralytic, carried by four of them. Since they could not get him to Jesus because of the crowd, they made an opening in the roof above Jesus and, after digging through it, lowered the mat the paralysed man was lying on. When Jesus saw their faith, he said to the paralytic, 'Son, your sins are forgiven.'

Now some teachers of the law were sitting there, thinking to themselves, 'Why does this fellow talk like that? He's blaspheming! Who can forgive sins but God alone?'

Immediately Jesus knew in his spirit that this was what they were thinking in their hearts, and he said to them, 'Why are you thinking these things? Which is easier: to say to the paralytic, "Your sins are forgiven," or to say, "Get up, take your mat and walk"? But that you may know that the Son of Man has authority on earth to forgive sins . . .' He said to the paralytic, 'I tell you, get up, take your mat and go home.'

(Mark 2:1–11)

This story always amazes me. Think about it carefully, and it's clear that the bizarre nature of the encounter carries an equally powerful message. In Matthew's version of the story the house in question was owned by a Levite, so this was an audience with some of the more respected members of society. As they sat there, politely listening to the man they couldn't quite work out, little did they know that a bunch of oiks were about to ruin the whole meeting AND get blessed by the Son of God for their troubles. What starts out with a little dust in the air soon ends up with the ceiling falling on their heads and a paralytic man being lowered down on a mat.

Now they took a huge risk there. Could you imagine if it hadn't worked out? The owner of the house would have been totally justified in beating their heads in. Imagine his embarrassment as society's elite gathered in his front room only to be subject to a bizarre terrorist healing attack. Thankfully Jesus' reaction was a little less predictable: the Bible says that when he saw their faith he said to the man,

'Your sins are forgiven . . . get up, take your mat and walk.'
What does it mean when it says, 'Jesus saw their faith'?
Did he see faith written on their foreheads? Did he see a
look of faith on their faces? What is an expression of faith,
anyway? How do you get one? I think what Jesus saw was
a hole in the roof. He saw what their faith had inspired
them to do: an act of incredible foolishness inspired by their
belief that Jesus could help them.

The stories of Jesus' time on earth are littered with similar
examples of people who have believed in him and acted on
their belief. The centurion believed so strongly that Jesus
would heal his servant that he didn't even need Jesus to
visit. The woman with the haemorrhage who touched Jesus'
cloak expected something to happen. Peter and John said
to the paralysed man at the gate Beautiful, in Acts chapter
3, 'Rise up, take your mat and walk.' What they all have in
common is faith, but not just faith as a feeling, or even as a
thought: in each case it is a motivator that initiates action.

As I learned at school, a verb is a doing word: faith is a verb.

Genesis chapters 12 to 22 describe Abraham as being a believer in God whose faith was credited to him as right-eousness. In other words, the way that he lived his life, acting on a belief that God was Almighty God, made God extremely happy. Because he believed in God, Abraham left his home for a place in which he was a stranger; because he believed in God, he believed that he would have a son. Thankfully (for us) this doesn't mean that Abraham lived a supercharged problem-free life; sleeping with Hagar could be seen as a 'low point', for example. However, he maintained his belief in God, making bold decisions and brave sacrifices because of that belief. In Abraham's case the presence of faith did not mean the absence of doubt.

Being a youth worker, I am always keen to keep up with the 'kidz'. That's why I wear tracksuits and surf the Web. Recently I was just hanging around the Yahoo site when I decided to search for someone I had heard of called Blondin, who made his name as an incredibly gifted tightrope walker. I ended up at two sites: first at *Encyclopaedia Britannica*, and second at one that told people how to become a Christian. Here's what I read:

Blondin: pseudonym of JEAN-FRANÇOIS GRAVE-LET (b. 28 Feb. 1824, Saint-Omer, Fr., d. 19 Feb. 1897, London), tightrope walker and acrobat who owed his celebrity and fortune to his feat of crossing Niagara Falls on a tightrope 1,100 feet (335 metres) long, 160 feet above the water.

It's about believing: The tightrope-walking Blondin was walking a rope across Niagara Falls. After crossing to the other side the crowds cheered him on. Blondin asked the crowd, 'Do you believe I can walk across with a wheelbarrow?'

The crowds cheered, 'We believe! We believe!'

Blondin replied, 'Do you believe I can do it with a man inside the barrow?'

At this the crowd broke into an uproar, and with passion they shouted, 'WE BELIEVE, WE BELIEVE!'

At this Blondin asked, 'Who, then, will volunteer to be that man?' The crowd became silent. No one volunteered!

If we are going to believe Jesus and what he says as being true, then we need to be prepared to hop into HIS barrow and trust our life fully to him. After all, that's what believing is about.

Now I'm not going to go on some trip about how the *Encyclopaedia Britannica* is missing the point, but I do think that the second section is far more revealing than the first. Those people who watched, applauded and refused to get in the wheelbarrow exercised a shallow faith that gave in to their fears for their own lives. That's not the sort of faith that we see exhibited in the Bible: instead we see countless examples of people who are willing to believe in God in spite of worries about themselves.

Face it, though, most of us wouldn't trust Blondin to give us a ride over Niagara Falls, and similarly most of us get a little shy when we feel one of those 'Divine Opportunities' coming our way. Our reaction is nothing new: when writing to the early Church, James pointed out that, 'You believe that there is one God. Good! Even the demons believe that – and shudder.' There is a long queue of people who 'Believe In God', but the one that really matters is the queue marked '. . . And Are Prepared To Do Something About It'. The praise of the spectators 160 feet below meant nothing to Blondin when they refused to trust him. The praise of God is worthless if we aren't prepared to 'hop', as the Internet Evangelist so beautifully puts it, 'into his barrow'.

How do you get faith?

Method One: ask. Like the man said, 'Lord, I believe. Help my unbelief' (Mark 9:24). Faith is a gift, and like all gifts we shouldn't feel bad about asking God for it. As we've already seen, faith is one of those gifts that is a response to him, and God being who he is he may well respond to a request for a top-up with a chance to practise. I can remember once hearing someone give the 'I want to believe, but I just don't have the faith' line. Days later they had heard the gospel, something had clicked and before they knew it they were faced with a chance to use faith. This may not happen to everyone, which is why some people hear the gospel and it leaves them cold.

Method two: through the word. There is a verse in Romans (10:17) which explains that 'faith comes from hearing the message, and the message is heard through the word of God'. At times just hearing the gospel preached can fire people up with faith to commit their lives. It seems that the Church is beginning to rediscover how to preach the gospel through works and deeds (a pivotal part of our faith), but it is important that because of this we don't reject proclaiming the gospel through words. Like many aspects of our faith, the secret is in the balance. As Paul understood, there is a power in the gospel and a power in proclaiming Jesus.

There is a second part to the connection between faith and the word, and it applies perhaps more to those who have already made a commitment. The Bible is full of inspirational and interactive stuff. At times we may get excited by a passage written by someone else that seems to describe our situation exactly. At other times the stories of

other people are like dynamite. When I read the stories of
God's faithfulness to Abraham, Moses and David it inspires
me. I think, 'I want to be like that. I want my life to be like
that.' When I read the Acts of the Apostles and I see the
faith of the first Christians, I think, 'Wow, this is the same
God!' That's why it's so important that we read the word.
We're bombarded all our lives with things that would
undermine our faith, but here in front of us is the last word
in practical advice.

The opposition to faith

Faith is all about our response to God, and our own personal faith will be as individual and unique as the very
character of the creator. We've all been through our own
experiences, doubts, insecurities and pains, and these will
make for our own stumbling blocks. My faith will be different from your faith, just as my pain is different from yours.
However, the wisdom of God is available to us, and through
it we can understand ourselves a little better and learn to
deal with it. A childhood full of disappointments and let-
downs will inevitably change you. As early promises of toys
and treats are made, they are believed with an innocence
and faith. A few broken promises down the line and the
response changes to, 'Yeah, I'll take that with a pinch of
salt.' The pain of the early disappointments teaches a new
reaction, one that means you don't get hurt. Perhaps it's
not surprising that we can carry these attitudes over from
our childhood into our relationship with God, suspiciously
eyeing up his promises. But as with all living things, our
healing takes time, and our emotions are especially fragile.
For God to be a living force in our lives he needs us to
respond to him. Through the stories and examples of his
character that we find in the Bible, we can begin to trust
him, begin to see that his promises are solid and for real,
unlike those thrown at us like sweets to quieten us down.

When I became a Christian there was an illustration of a train that everybody seemed to use. The engine was called Facts, the first carriage Faith and the second Feelings. For the whole thing to work the engine had to be in front, pulling the carriages. If our faith is following the facts, then the feelings will follow behind. If we decide to put our feelings up front, then the train goes nowhere. The 1970s were full of things like that.

Maybe you find it hard to believe that when you've confessed your sins, God has forgiven you. Despite your prayers you feel dirty, unclean and guilty. If you choose (and sometimes it's a difficult choice to make) to put your faith in your feelings, then you'll believe that you are unforgiven. But if you decide to look at the facts and see in Scripture that Jesus died for all men and women, that his blood is sufficient to cover all sin, you will find it a lot easier to believe that you are forgiven. It may take a while, but the feelings will follow. This can happen in any situation, although I'm not saying that it's easy. But as Jesus said, 'You shall know the truth and the truth will set you free.'

How do we grow in faith?

As with much of the Christian life, there seems to be a lot of false propaganda going around. Faith comes in for more than its fair share as we are frequently confronted with the assumption that having true faith means never having any doubts. As John Wimber said, 'Faith is spelt R-I-S-K' – if we are not prepared to risk failure, we will find it hard to develop our faith. If you are about to risk your whole reputation, career or life, you would have to be a robot not to think twice; you are bound to have doubts. Deciding to do something for the first time, stepping out of the comfort zone and saying, 'Either God's going to come, or I've had it' is a scary place to be, but there's none better. Some of us never hop into the wheelbarrow, and so faith remains malnourished and underdeveloped. Thankfully, help is at hand, and all we need to do is say yes. To grow in faith is to begin to live like that, and the more you do it the more you grow.

Faith is important to the whole of our lives: even prophecy is linked to faith, as it says in Scripture that we prophesy according to our faith. In fact you can swap the word 'prophesy' here for all sorts of things. We love according to our faith. We are vulnerable according to our faith. We forgive according to our faith. We see miracles happen according to our faith. We venture out and do great exploits according to our faith. Returning to Hebrews 11, we read that 'by faith . . .' all manner of biblical exploits were carried out. We too will grow in faith by stepping out in faith; like muscles, the more we exercise our faith, the more it grows. That doesn't mean it ever gets easy, because, unlike with muscles, there are no steroids.

Practically we have found much of this out at Soul Survivor. The first time we ever put on a festival we were gripped by the fear of two simple questions: 'Will anyone come?' and 'Will we go bankrupt?' (for your interest the answers were 'yes' and 'not quite'). We had doubts right from the start, but did that mean we lacked faith? The mark of that would have been if we had called it off. Obviously faith has to be a response to God's word, and with the festival we believed that God had told to us to do it. A few years later we bought a warehouse for our local church in Watford. The building cost £300,000 and we spent another £90,000 doing it up. At the time we were a church of about fifty young people – fifty poor young people. We had neither the money nor the prospect of getting the money (legally), but we believed that God said he would look after us and that he would provide the money (legally). So far he has been doing just that. It has been an anxious couple of

years, and at times we have wondered, 'How are you going
to do it now, Lord?', but we have managed to keep going,
totally boosted by the belief that God is powerful and
trustworthy.

Yet what happens when you put your faith in the Lord
and it doesn't work out? Let's be honest: it happens, and
we are left asking why. When Joseph dreamed of his
brothers bowing down before him, wasn't it from God? In
the end the dream turned out to be correct, but Joseph had
messed up the timing. We once promoted a tour and lost
£14,000. We were upset. Had we heard God wrong? Was it
wrong to do the tour in the first place?

The truth is that God will have his will, God will do
what he wants anyway. He cared more for me than he did
for the tour not losing money. He was more interested in
what he did in Joseph than what he did through Joseph.
He put him through all that suffering and Joseph came
out of it not bitter, but better. When he met his brothers
he said, 'Don't worry, you didn't do this to me. God sent
me ahead of you, that through me you might be saved.
What you did you meant for harm, but God meant it
for good.'

Many years before that, when Joseph was in the middle
of his nightmare, he chose to trust God. When Pharaoh said,
'I hear you're good on dreams,' common sense would have
told Joseph to leave well alone and say, 'No, Pharaoh, I
used to be into dreams but it hasn't done me any good so
I've given up on that one.' Instead, he said, 'No, God gives
the interpretation to dreams, I will ask God.' He continued
to trust in what God had given him. The only way you get
to succeed is by risking failure in the Christian faith. Many
of us don't succeed because we aren't willing to risk
failure, and we decide to settle for mediocrity. Faith is
continuing to trust God in adversity, still believing him
when things go wrong. Without it you just get bitter.

Without it you just go nowhere. Faith, like yeast in beer, is
what makes Christianity work.

Live it!

I sometimes wonder whether faith is like a switch that can
only ever be turned to 'on' or 'off'. Talking to people who
don't consider themselves to be believers in God, it certainly
seems that way, and I suspect that there are more than a
few of you reading this who have heard the old line about
how 'I wish I could have faith but I just can't seem to
manage it'. I wish I had some neat little answer that tied it
all up for them, a few choice words that would have the
scales falling from their eyes and see them falling to their
knees crying 'Yes, now I believe'. But it just doesn't seem to
work like that. Faith is not a label, an artificial limb or a left
turn at the next set of lights. It's not even a question of
having it or not having it, for, like the father of the boy said
in Mark 9:24, there can be times when we all need a little
more. So faith, it would seem, is not something that is either
on or off: perhaps it's more like a sliding scale, one on which
we could all do with going further along towards a fuller
relationship with God.

Task

Abraham's faith marked him out for special attention from
God. What ways could your life show your faith in God?
Start by making a list of areas that you find difficult to let
go of, for example worrying about money, work or friends.
Make the list as detailed as you like, perhaps by writing
down examples of specific times when you've felt that

you've been far away from God on a particular issue. Pray through each of the items on your list, asking God to show you practical ways of how you can trust him more.

6

Chocolate and other evils

(a chapter about temptation)

Like the European Union and Manchester United, warfare
is one of those topics on which opinion is well and truly
divided. Many follow the path marked 'Ignore It', while
others plump for the one called 'Adore It'. There has been
many a time when I sweated away my teenage years pic-
turing myself as a heavenly Van Damme getting stuck into
a little one-on-one with some present problem. At other
times I would walk along the Christian path, blissfully
unaware that I was in the middle of the most violent of
storms. A big fan of C.S. Lewis, I have managed to be
living proof of his theory that the Devil's two main plans
of attack are to get us either to be obsessed with him or in
a state of complete unbelief. So how do we do it? How do
we live the life without the obsessions or the ignorance?
And if we do manage to work it out, what's the benefit to
us anyway?

Nehemiah and the wall

We start out in the book of Nehemiah, which, being one of
the less well-known Old Testament books, has the added
advantage of making this chapter seem very spiritual. (Now
might be a good time for you to pick up your Bible and
turn to the book of Nehemiah, just to check that I'm not
lying.) Nehemiah tells his story, and throughout it we can
see three classic ways in which Satan attacks the people of
God. In fact, so classic are the attacks on Nehemiah that

even today we seem to experience the same ones in the same order. Spooky. Through his story we can see that for much of the time warfare is about resisting temptation and focusing on God rather than trying to dismantle the enemy's kingdom ourselves.

Nehemiah was cupbearer to the King of Babylon at the time of the Jewish exile, and lived in the citadel of Susa (the winter palace). One day Hanani, one of his brothers, arrives from Jerusalem and tells him all about life in Jerusalem. The situation is bad: without decent walls the city lies in ruins; even though Ezra has been rebuilding it, every time progress is made it is destroyed by their enemies. Time and time again Jerusalem has been plundered, leaving it a pale reflection of the grand city it once was. Nehemiah's response to Hanani's news is quick and simple: 'When I heard these things, I sat down and wept. For some days I mourned and fasted and prayed before the God of heaven.'

As we said in the chapter on prayer, any work of God starts with weeping. It doesn't start with forming a committee, devising an action plan or chanting 'Go For It' twenty times an hour. This may sound a little foolish, but as Western Christians we're dead keen on using our Practical-DIY-Get-Up-And-Go-Let-Me-Sort-It-God skills and not so chuffed when it comes to sitting down and letting God take the lead. Practical problems don't always need our practical solutions.

Before being sent out to get his hands dirty, Nehemiah had his heart well and truly broken by God. Too often we try and go out and DO SOMETHING because we've been inspired by a talk, a sermon or a book, but the trouble is we're going out without having been broken, we're leaving without full preparation for the journey. Many times we turn back halfway, disillusioned, disenchanted or just plain distracted. Now I know that all sounds very neat and tidy, with its three D's and all that, but letting God take the lead has to be the best way of making sure that you're doing the right thing.

Having wept, mourned and fasted for some days, Nehemiah prays. What he says to God is an unusual yet fantastic prayer: he begins by praising him, and follows with a confession of the sins of his people. He confesses that he too has been a part of the wickedness and disobedience. For all we can tell, Nehemiah was a very righteous man who could easily have distanced himself from those who had done the real sinning. Instead he identifies with the people and avoids being patronising. In a way his words are an early illustration of the saying that the preaching of the gospel is simply one beggar telling another where to find food; we are all equal in our falling short of God's standards.

A while later, Nehemiah packs up and heads off to Jerusalem with the blessing of his king. The trip would have taken three and a half months by camel, which means that he would have been forced to cut his ties with Susa.

Arriving at Jerusalem, he checks the city out for a while and eventually lets the people in on his plan. He gets them fired up with the vision and they all begin work on rebuilding the wall. Once they start they come under attack from their enemies, attacks of the type that we experience today.

First we are introduced to Sanballat the Horonite and his mate Tobiah the Ammonite, who happens to be one of those sort of people who, at school, would have been mouthing off next to the school bully, too puny to fight his own battles. He gets stuck in with an early round of ridicule in chapter 4 (verse 3), giving it a load of mouth about their wall not being strong enough even for a fox to climb up on it. Like him, the enemy often attacks us with ridicule over the things about which we are most insecure. These subtle attacks get us where it hurts: instead of making up something that is plainly untrue, we get hit with the thought,

'Of course, I couldn't do anything great for God. After all, I don't pray nearly enough and my Bible is covered in dust.' Having had thousands of years in which to work on this technique, the enemy seems to be doing pretty well at lying. Jesus said that Satan is a liar and the father of lies. That means he's a very good liar. His best lies are half-truths. I've never suffered from the sudden panic that God could never use me because I'm anorexic: look at me and you don't see anorexic. What I do go for, though, is the line about me being disorganised, forgetful and a complete nightmare to work with. By feeding us a line that is partly true, the Devil has a much better chance of us swallowing the whole thing.

Look at Nehemiah: he was previously a cupbearer, so he probably hadn't won many awards for wall construction. The joke about the fox was probably a bit too close for comfort, and could easily have got him down. Instead Nehemiah's reaction was spot on: choosing not to argue about the merits of his particular building technique, he turned to God in prayer.

The second attack is the not-so-subtle full-frontal assault that we read about in verses 7 to 11. The enemies club together and decide that the rebuilding is something that should be stopped immediately. They go so far as to threaten to murder the workers. At times we may encounter opposition: perhaps someone may react to us with an unexpected and unreasonable level of anger. It may come from outside the church or from within; it may be the result of hanging out with people from school or starting something new in the youth group. Satan may even send illness to get us really freaked, and if he gets his way we give up, thinking that The Blessing isn't flowing and we are not doing what God wants. This is a rubbish excuse. Just take a look at the Bible and it's easy to see that the signs of persecution (shipwrecks, imprisonment and torture) were for Paul the signs that he was in exactly the right place. God does want the best for us, but the best is not always the easiest – the best is being in the centre of our Father's will.

What Nehemiah and his countrymen did in verse 9 was another great response to an attack. They prayed *and* they posted a guard. They didn't just do the spiritual thing, nor did they lean exclusively on the practical – they found the balance. As D.L. Moody said, when faced with a certain situation we should pray as if the entire outcome depended on God, and work as if it depended on us. With such a good response to the second attack, though, the third is not far off.

Chapter 6, and the work is all done apart from a little door-hanging. It isn't hard to imagine that this collective of abused, oppressed and under-resourced builders would be feeling a little tired at this point, wide open to temptation. The enemies spread a few rumours and offered a meeting and a chance to compromise on Nehemiah's earlier position. Nehemiah, refusing to give in, sees their attack for what it is and sends them away, praying for more strength to finish the job. Compromise for Nehemiah would have meant throwing away the potential of a mighty work of God. Accepting second best might leave us with an easier ride in the short term, but ultimately it's a waste of a life.

Unlike Nehemiah, you could say that the American televangelists who fell so publicly in the early 1990s compromised with sin. The actual point of compromise may have been the sin that brought them down, or it may have happened long before that, when they did away with the need for accountability.

My dark sin

I have an addiction. Since my early teens, when I was first introduced to it at school, I have been involved in a violent battle with cake. I have suffered attacks from all manner of confectionery and pastries, yet the one that grips my soul the tightest is the legendary Triple Chocolate Surprise. I make no apologies for what I am about to describe, though I hope that it may comfort a few.

One evening I returned to my flat, having been away at an event. I was feeling tired and low, once again going through the turbulence of returning to normality after being 'looked after' so well for the previous few days. Having unpacked (using my usual two-second Open And Tip method) I sat down and looked about me. I surveyed my home, feeling surprised that as a reflection of my character the flat seemed to focus more heavily on the chaotic and disorganised bits of me rather than the highly intellectual and stylish bits that I knew were there in abundance. Midway through a thought about how much more dust it would take before I could use my coffee table as a mattress, my eyes wandered and landed on the fridge. My heart began to beat faster as I remembered what lay inside: a cake so rich and full of chocolate that when I bought it I had found it necessary to make an excuse to the shop assistant about it being 'purely for medical research'. I had not yet touched the cake, and it had been settling down in the fridge for a couple of days. It was such a beautiful piece of craftsmanship that I decided it would be good just to open the fridge door and gaze upon it, to take in the full glory. I decided I would only look.

What followed may be hard to believe, but I say nothing but the truth. It spoke to me. I remember the words as if they were uttered yesterday: 'Hello, Mike,' said the cake. Somewhat taken aback, I returned the greeting and we exchanged pleasantries. I invited the cake to join me on the kitchen table for a little tête-à-tête before bedtime. Slowly I took it out of the fridge and sat down opposite. Delicate beads of moisture formed on the sides as it reacted to the heat of the room. Reacting to the size of the cake, I began to dribble.

Soon I had transferred 4.35kg of high-density chocolate cake from the packaging to my gut. I began by cutting myself a millimetre-thin slice, and followed through with a frenzied hand-to-mouth session that was all over in five minutes. I was not quite sure how I felt immediately – I suppose I was overawed by the beauty of the cake – but it was as I went to bed that I began to feel a tad off-colour. As I lay down I was aware of a strange sensation, one that reminded me of a working model I had once seen of Mount Krakatoa. And so began the worst night's sleep (if it can even be called that) that I have ever experienced.

As I lay in my bed, watching the room brighten with the sun, I reflected on the cause of my fall from grace. Was it, I asked myself, when I took up the cake's kind offer of running my finger around the rim to taste the cream? Was it when I cut that first slice? Was it when I swapped the teaspoon for the dessertspoon, thus enabling me to get more in each time? Was it when I gave up on cutlery altogether and used my hands to shove the cake in? Then the truth came to me: the cause of my physical agony was the opening of the fridge door. Once I had the cake in view, there was no stopping me and my problems had begun. Now, of course, you know that I am not just talking about chocolate cake here. This applies to all tempting morsels: pie, profiteroles, ice cream, custard and sex. So be warned – whatever your poison is, don't open the fridge door.

Elijah meets God

Elijah was another one who came under a few attacks. Having sorted out the 450 prophets of Baal on the top of Mount Carmel, securing his title as Undisputed Hard And Holy Man Of The Year, we find him running away from a woman called Jezebel. He sits under a broom tree in the middle of the desert, wants to die and is in what can only be described as a big strop. How could that happen to one so tough? The similarities between Elijah and me may not be immediately obvious, but I know how he feels. I know what it's like to wake up and feel like the richest man in the world – who could be happier? I have great friends, I get paid to do a job I love and I get to stand on platforms looking important – and at other times I think I've got absolutely nothing. I'll sit in my flat and run through my list: I'm thirty-nine and I'm a youth worker; in a few months I'll be forty and will have reached my sell-by date – or maybe I already have and no one's told me. I'm single and may never marry – who do I have that would be utterly devastated if I died? There may never be little Pilavachis running around the place. What am I going to do with the rest of my life?

Most of us know what this feels like. Elijah went through something that many of us experience when we return from Soul Survivor, Spring Harvest or some great meeting. Suddenly the adrenaline stops flowing and we panic. Elijah had experienced a De Luxe Move Of God and was left feeling like a slug. God's response was not perhaps one that you would expect; he told Elijah to sleep and sent an angel with bread and water to tend to him, proving that God's spirituality is a lot more practical than ours. Not feeling like a spiritual giant when we are knackered is not a sin, it's a reality.

Second, God took Elijah to a cleft in the mountain and laid on a display of raw power – an earthquake, a hurricane and a fire. However, God didn't choose to speak through them; instead he used a gentle whisper. When Elijah heard it he put on his cloak and went back the way he came. The significance of this verse is huge. Through the experience God taught Elijah that life isn't about the earthquakes of Soul Survivor, the winds of Greenbelt or the fire of Spring Harvest, but about finding him in the ordinary and the mundane. When we have no big spiritual events acting as our supports it's vital that we can still hear his voice. Instead of having a relationship with his children through a collection of spiritual highs, God wants to be our life source.

Be sensible

There are times when I go home after a meeting and I feel dreadful. Sleep is an impossibility and listening to the BBC World Service is my only entertainment. I may pace around the flat for a while or try and read a book, but generally I'm too caught up in feeling bad about myself to concentrate on anything other than my sad life. I need to learn to find God in that place and pour out my heart to him. I can also learn to anticipate when I am going to feel low and vulnerable to attack. A policeman friend of mine once gave me the best advice that he knew: in a conflict, run. There's nothing wrong with avoiding those situations in which we know that the enemy is going to have a good chance at knocking us off balance.

Turn off the darkness

For some, perhaps, this idea of focusing on God and avoiding the attacks may not seem much like warfare. Where is the battle against darkness? Where are the encounters with the demons? Paul experienced his fair share of opposition; you could say he was a seasoned warrior. For all his experience he chose to find the balance between ignorance and obsession. When he wrote to the church at Ephesus he mentioned that ours is not a fight against flesh and blood but against the 'principalities and powers, against the rulers of this present darkness'. He listed the weapons with which to fight, yet when he arrived there (a city which was a centre of demonic activity; even the economy was based on demonology) he didn't hide himself in a room and charge up on a little one-on-one with the local principalities or powers. Instead, he spread the kingdom by preaching the gospel and healing the sick. Demons were cast out, but he concentrated on building the Church rather than dismantling the enemy.

Watford has a history of disunity between churches, and when we started Soul Survivor Watford we anticipated a fair amount of hostility. From one couple, though, we got the exact opposite: instead of warning people off about us, Gordon and Rachel Hickson (the pastors of Watford Community Church) told all their young people to come and visit us. 'I may well lose them to you,' Gordon told me, 'but I don't care.' A little confused, we asked him to explain.

He told us that when they arrived in Watford they saw all the opposition between the churches. They decided that they were going to live in the opposite spirit, determined that they were going to be generous and bless all the other churches. Since then the churches have come together, united against the enemy. That's warfare.

Imagine going to live in Soho. Instead of moving into a flat and combating the powers of sexual perversion and immorality by shadow-boxing the demons from your front room, wouldn't it be better to live in the opposite spirit? Where people are greedy, you could be generous, where there is immorality you could be pure, and where there is an absence of hope you could instil self-worth and pride. That too would be warfare.

We need to read the Bible – the truth – in order to resist the enemy's lies. In Luke 4 we read of the temptation of Jesus in the desert. He was tempted by the Devil, and he was tempted when he was at his weakest. I struggle if I have fasted between breakfast and lunch; Jesus had been at it for forty days. He was hungry. He was tired. After forty days in the desert he would have been in desperate need of comfort. The Devil chose his moment. (The Devil always chooses his moments.) He tempted Jesus at his weakest. If I had been in Jesus' place, I would have thought, 'I've been spiritual for forty whole days. One loaf of Hovis won't do any harm.'

Jesus answered, 'It is written, man does not live on bread alone.' There came two other temptations, to each of which Jesus answered, 'It is written.' One of the biggest helps in resisting temptation is to know the word, to live the word and to let the word live in you. It would have been very difficult for Jesus to have said, 'It is written,' if he hadn't known what had been written. In John's gospel Jesus told the disciples that, when needed, the Holy Spirit would remind them of everything that he had told them. That promise is for us. The Holy Spirit can't remind us if we don't know it in the first place. In Ephesians 6 we are told that the sword of the Spirit is the word of God. We need to be equipped with the sword of the Spirit; knowing the word gives us a reference point outside our feelings when the temptations are strong.

Perhaps God could have done things a little differently two thousand years ago. Perhaps he could have had a heavenly battle against the darkness, but instead he chose to send down some purity, send down some light. In his life, Jesus offers a perfect model of living in a counter-cultural way; while at times he confronted the enemy head on, for the most part he spread love, forgiveness and relationship with God.

Live it!

Your problem may not be with cake as such, but we all have our areas of weakness. I know my 'little sins' often cause me to mess up just a bit, but you know, they don't really hurt anyone, do they?

And this is my problem: I downgrade the seriousness of sin and allow the temptation to get a foot in the doorway. Life, it would seem, is difficult, but I can make it slightly easier if I ease off on the rules just a bit. OK, so I know that it's uncool, oppressive and totally at odds with our 'if it feels good do it' culture, but we need to be wise to temptation, we must be strong when attacked. But how? What can we do to help us live the life without resorting to the twin extremes of complete paranoia or total ignorance?

Think back to the story of Nehemiah: part of getting on with the job in hand of rebuilding the walls was to weep, mourn and fast for days. This meant that Nehemiah went out with his and his people's own weakness very much in mind. Now you might think such manner of preparation odd for so prestigious a project, and it's true; Nehemiah isn't giving himself what you would call a classic pep-talk. And that's the beauty. Nehemiah knew that in his own strength he could achieve nothing and on his own merit he deserved even less. But this was God's gig and Nehemiah wasn't going to get in the way. From day one onwards, he allowed God to take control.

And here's where we bring back the puddings: by undermining the seriousness of my sin, by opening that fridge door, by allowing just one more slice, I miss the point of all this. Temptation becomes all about me and my appetites. God? Well, it often feels like it has precious little to do with him. How wrong I am.

Task 1

Think about what your areas of weakness are. Are you feeling brave? Write down on a piece of paper one thing that you'd love God to help you deal with. Fold it up and place it in front of you. Are you worried that someone might see it? Scary to know that your secret could so easily be out, isn't it? But can you really have secrets from God? Are there things we honestly think that we can hide from our Maker? Take time to confess the ways in which you have fallen down. Ask him to help you change. Accept his forgiveness. Get rid of the piece of paper.

Task 2

Look back over Nehemiah's story in the book of Ezra and think further about the way he responded to temptation.

How would you summarise the N-Plan guide to resisting attack? Can you put it into practice in your own life?

7
Everybody loves a lover

(a chapter about being family)

If the first and greatest commandment is that we love the
Lord our God with all our heart, soul, mind, and strength,
then the second greatest is not far off: that we love our
neighbour as ourselves. Jesus knew that we would probably
need things explained a little, so he carried on, making it
into a whole new commandment: 'My command is this:
Love each other as I have loved you. Greater love has no
one than this, that he lay down his life for his friends. You
are my friends if you do what I command' (John 15:12–14).
The command suddenly becomes even harder to stick to as
Jesus throws in the bit about being as good at loving as
him. It makes me wonder why Jesus felt the need to give a
new commandment to the disciples just before he died. It
seems that the answer is that he knew that the Church
wouldn't survive if the new Christians (his disciples) did
not love one another with something approaching the same
depth and commitment that he had shown them.

It took me quite a while to realise that the bits in the
Bible that are labelled as commands are not just the optional
extras that you can take or leave as the mood suits. I spent
many years forgiving people about as often as I washed
out my lunch box. Due to a particularly bad bout of internal
fungus, I realised one day that Jesus gave commands because he meant his people to do what he said. If we know
what's good for us, we will try and be his disciples – taking
the commands that he gave the first twelve as our own.

Yet what does it mean to love one another as Jesus loved
us? The culture from which Jesus came is far removed from

ours, so how can we find the connection between his actions and our possibilities? In order to understand this we need to return to Jesus' initial comments about loving one another. He explains himself more fully by saying, 'Greater love has no one than this, that he lay down his life for his friends.' On one level Jesus was talking about what he was about to do: to go to the cross on behalf of his friends and loved ones. But it wasn't just about going to the cross as an isolated act of kindness. Jesus took up his cross long before he had been captured. He continually laid down his life by preferring the disciples. While it may not result in crucifixion, we are called to lay down our lives for each other, putting others first, with our own needs and preferences taking second place. Even though Jesus was the Son of God, he treated his disciples not only as equals, but even as superiors. He calls us to be servants of one another as he was a servant to us.

A Guide To Loving Each Other
Like Jesus Loved Us (in four parts)

Part 1: To be vulnerable

The first way that Jesus loved the disciples was by being vulnerable before them. Vulnerability is a hard word for Western people to accept. Many of us, particularly men from an English culture, have been brought up to think that the showing of emotion is as embarrassing as a fart on a train. We would rather spend our lives as prisoners to this way of living than share with others our grief, pain and fear. We seem to be taking our cue from the two Jameses (Bond and T. Kirk) and from Gallagher Jnr. Yet Jesus didn't live like that; his wasn't a model of Lone Ranger Christianity. We shouldn't look to the examples of emotional constipation; instead, Jesus showed another way, gathering his people around him and sacrificing every part of himself for them.

Jesus was not only vulnerable, he was willing to show his vulnerability by his actions. He not only felt things deeply, he was willing for people to see what he felt. He wept over Jerusalem and he wept over his friend Lazarus. It amazes me, not so much that Jesus wept over the city and over a man, but that he allowed people to see him weep. Many of us do our weeping in private, cleaning up and putting on a smile when we're in public. Jesus showed his vulnerability in the garden of Gethsemane when he cried out to God in anguish. There was vulnerability on the cross when he allowed people to strip him naked, laugh at him and taunt him.

Many of us are afraid of being vulnerable because of one simple equation: vulnerability = pain. There is no way around the fact that if you make yourself vulnerable, you will be hurt. But what makes us so special that we should have an easier deal than Jesus? He called us to live lives of vulnerability with each other, and that means risking pain and hurt as he did. As followers of Christ we are meant to engage with one another as he did, because he did.

There are three pictures of the Church that I have heard and thought about. Colin Urquhart had the first one years ago. He felt that churchgoers are like snooker balls, who come out of their pockets on a Sunday, bounce off each other and say, 'Clickety-click, Amen,' before returning down the holes. Next Sunday there they are again, bouncing and clicking, giving it a bit of 'Amen' and then returning to pocketland. Then one Sunday the church gets charismatic and the Christians get filled with the Spirit. From now on they come out of their pockets and say, 'Clickety-click, amen, praise the Lord, hallelujah!' and get back down the holes. They are still hard on the outside, despite being filled with the Spirit on the inside. Sadly, some churches are like that, full of fired-up people who refuse to be vulnerable with each other.

An evangelist from Argentina called Juan Carlos Ortis had another picture of the Church, but this time it was of how it should be. He called it Mashed Potato Love. God takes a whole load of spuds, hard and individual, peels them, boils them and then mashes them together. That's how God wants his people to be: not individual hard spuds, but one glorious mound of creamy mash. In many ways it's a wonderful picture, but it does give the idea that we lose our individuality by being part of the body.

A picture I prefer is one that a friend of mine had some years ago. He saw a honeycomb made up of hundreds of six-sided cells, with each cell being in direct contact with five others. If one cell in the honeycomb was damaged, all the others around would be affected. My friend felt that this was how the Church should be, maintaining individuality yet encouraging a strong bond between each of the members. So, as in a honeycomb, if one cell laughs the others should feel the vibrations. If one cell cries, the others should all get wet. This is what Paul understood when he wrote to the Romans and advised them to 'rejoice with those who rejoice; mourn with those who mourn' (Rom. 12:15). The unity between us as Christians is supposed to be that strong.

Part 2: To forgive

The second way that Jesus loved his disciples was by forgiving them. Jesus tells us to love one another as he loved us, so we need to forgive as Jesus forgave. The chances are that this will become a regular occurrence, for as we make ourselves vulnerable to others we come across the old 'vulnerability = pain' rule again, as people let us down. Having been hurt, the only healthy reaction that we can put into place is to forgive.

I have found forgiveness the hardest part of being a Christian. Inasmuch as the English are born with the legacy of the stiff upper lip, we Greeks come into the world with the words 'Never Forgive' imprinted on our hearts. I think I managed to work at it a little bit, and soon found that when a relative stranger hurt me it was not too difficult to grant them my cleansing forgiveness. However, if a friend does something to hurt me it's a very different story. Normally my first reaction is simple, but effective: I decide not to forgive. I follow that up with a swift dose of ignorance, trying as hard as I can to put the situation out of mind. The trouble starts when I end up in a worship meeting. I may be in the middle of singing a tender song to Jesus when all of a sudden I start thinking about that Judas, the one that hurt me. Again I try and wipe them from my memory, but it seems as though God is saying, 'You can't worship me unless you forgive.' A struggle usually follows, and eventually I end up giving in (the odds *are* slightly stacked against me, after all). Having forgiven them I feel better, the awkward feeling in the pit of my stomach being replaced with a little peace and lovely, fluffy, bouncy thoughts.

This state usually lasts for about one minute. I remember why I had to forgive them in the first place and I'm back at square one, although this time feeling even more angry as they've fooled me into forgiving them beforehand. 'Forgive them again,' says the Lord. So I do and things are lovely, fluffy and bouncy again.

Until the next time I see them. If it happens to be out somewhere and everyone is having a laugh except them, crying in a corner on their own, then I find it surprisingly easy to maintain my high standard of forgiveness. But if they happen to be the centre of attention, that twisted feeling starts up in my stomach again and I can see no reason why I should let them off the hook. After all, I reason, if I did forgive them they would obviously not learn their lesson. If it wasn't for my sharp stings of correction, how would they ever grow? At times I feel like God's Ambassador, put on this earth to do the dirty work of showing people the consequences of their sin. God's reply is swift: 'Shut it – that's my job. Because I forgave you, you must forgive them.'

Perhaps my scenario is not so ridiculous, for one of the disciples once asked Jesus how many times we should forgive. He suggested the figure seven. I may be missing the point here, but what on earth made him think of seven? Apart from Matthew (the tax collector) and Judas, the other disciples were not very good at maths, and a man of that calibre would probably have been foxed by Jesus' answer: 'No, not seven times, seventy times seven' – which basically means we are to forgive all the time. We are supposed to forgive each person until the hurt goes away (not, as I used to think, 490 different people). If we are honest that can be a long time, but in sending his Son to the cross God gave us a clear answer to a simple question: how much do we deserve forgiveness?

We need to practise forgiveness, to learn how to continually forgive someone even though they might be a) unrepentant, b) unaware, or c) better-looking. Sadly, the consequence of not forgiving is that we become bitter and twisted as their fault becomes our problem. They may not be aware, or even care, that you want to kill them; the person that gets screwed up is you, and the relationship that gets most screwed up is the relationship between you and God.

Part 3: To serve

Jesus also showed his love for the disciples by choosing to serve them. There was one time when Jesus and the disciples arrived at a place having been out in the desert (John 13). It seems that the servants had the day off, and there was nobody around of low enough rank to get down and wash people's feet. Jesus took a towel and some water and got down on his knees and got on with the job. 'As I, your Lord and teacher, do this to you, you are to do it for one another,' he said.

This seemed like a great illustration of servanthood, and so one day I decided to re-create the moment with my youth group. We were away at the time, and the night before I prompted them as to what we were going to do the next day so that nobody would be embarrassed by whipping off their socks and suffocating everyone else with their scent. We had done a little homework and turned up prepared; we had plenty of hot water, clean towels, individual bowls and a lifetime's supply of Passion Fruit And Limestone Foot Cream. That morning everyone came downstairs and we split into pairs to wash each other's feet. We all were moved by the experience of having another person serving us in such a way, and then by returning the favour. We finished with a wise thought that I had prepared: 'Now that,' I said, 'is exactly what Jesus did two thousand years ago.'

A few days later I thought about my closing speech and realised that what we had done was nothing like what Jesus did two thousand years ago. Jesus didn't actually say to the disciples, 'I'm on wash duty tomorrow so make sure you all have a good scrub beforehand.' Nor did he say that he was about to produce a superb sermon illustration and it would be very much appreciated if they could all pay attention and not do anything silly to spoil it. There was a reason why the disciples sat around saying, 'I'm not doing the washing' – having been out in the desert their feet were hardly a vision of loveliness; sweat, mud, blood and turds would have been more like it. It was usually the job of the lowest servant, the one who amounted to nothing, yet this time Jesus put himself out.

There are all sorts of ways in which we can serve others. One of my favourite techniques is the Humble Yet Highly Visual. I believe that I could go head to head with the most servant-hearted of people as long as there was a good crowd to cheer me on. When I play to a heavenly audience of one, I find things a little harder work.

When I first joined St Andrew's Chorleywood I travelled there by train from my home in Harrow. This soon got round to being a pain and I was whingeing to my friend Chris about it. He suggested that we pray about it, and we asked God to find me somewhere to stay, if only for a short while. A few days later I had a call from two ladies in the church who asked me to flat-sit for them while they went on a six-week trip to New Zealand. I agreed, and was totally amazed. I was soon on the phone to Chris, telling him about this fantastic answer to prayer. He was really pleased too, and said it was great the way the Lord answers prayer.

I had a great time while they were away. I had just about managed to replace the £150 bottle of cognac (which I had used to pep up a tin of fruit salad) by the time they returned home, and we sat around and had a chat before I left. 'There's one thing that's been puzzling me,' I said, 'and that's why you asked me in the first place.'

'Didn't you know?' they replied. 'Chris suggested your name. He said you would make a great flat-sitter.'

That bowled me over. There was no way he would have let me know, and I found out by accident. If it had been me I would surely have turned on the charm with the old 'Oh please, it was nothing, you would have done the same for me. It was a bit of a sweat getting you the flat, mind you, but I persuaded them and put my name on the line for you.' There was nothing in it for Chris, just the simple act of being a servant. God works in a similar way; loving us because of his love, not because of the buzz he gets.

Part 4: To be honest

Jesus also loved his disciples by being honest with them. The verse in Ephesians that mentions speaking the truth in love (Eph. 4:15) is often misused to justify un-Christlike behaviour. At a church I used to go to there was one gentleman who seemed to make a habit of catching my eye and heading straight for me, releasing into the air the magic words, 'Now I say this in love, brother . . .' It was as if he thought the very words would turn whatever telling-off that followed into pearls of great wisdom. Far from having me fall to my knees in humbled privilege to have been enlightened by this Great Man of God, the 'I Say This In Love' warning had me on my knees faking a heart attack in the hope that he might leave well alone and prey on some-one else.

Thankfully the true meaning of the verse is a little differ-ent. To speak the truth in love means first of all to speak positive and affirming truth. I'm not talking about saying schmaltzy, honey-covered things like 'I think you're like a lovely little lamb and your bleating is like an angel's harp.' The truth is nothing if it is not honest. We find this hard to do – it seems to contradict our nature of being strong and independent, as if by acknowledging someone else's strength we admit our weakness.

On another occasion I was talking with my youth group about encouraging one another with things that were honest and true. To illustrate it each of them took a piece of paper and wrote their name at the top. They then passed the sheets around and wrote on each other's one thing that would be an encouragement.

This was the most buzzing thing we had ever done in the youth group. Bless them, I thought, these little ones obviously need affirming. I thanked God that I was mature enough not to need to take part. Then one of them called my bluff and asked me if I was joining in. For the sake of setting an example I joined in, fully intending just to glance at my sheet some time over the next few months. When everyone had finished writing, they took their sheets and read through the twenty-two reasons why they were liked.

The loudest lad in the group went into a corner and

stayed there for twenty minutes, reading and re-reading what was written on the paper. It was as if he was drinking it in. At the end he came up to me and asked if I could help him work out which person had written which comment. Even six months later they still had those pieces of paper, pinned on their noticeboard or stuck in their Bibles.

Bless them, I thought as they left, they obviously needed that. I then ran upstairs and tore open my piece of paper, reading it over and over, trying to work out which comment belonged to which person. None of us are too old, too mature or too secure to pass up on a bit of affirmation. We are meant to affirm others because it reflects the character of Jesus.

There is, though, another side to speaking the truth in love, because sometimes we all need a little guidance as we fumble our way along the path. There isn't much worse than hearing the hard truth about ourselves from an enemy, especially if they are good enemies, in which case they are bound to make sure that what they say really hurts. Infinitely preferable is hearing those home truths from a friend – as the proverb says, 'Faithful are the wounds of a friend.' Delivering the truth in this way doesn't mean slagging someone off once the all-purpose 'I say this in love . . .' tag has been added. Our words should come out of a caring and compassionate heart, the test of which is to ask: Do I enjoy pointing this 'problem' out to my friend? If the answer is yes, then you should keep quiet and go back to torturing fieldmice. If it hurts you to say it, then you care more about the person than you care about getting it off your chest. We receive correction much better from those who we know love us.

A helpful saying

It seems funny, but the things that stick with you from a talk are often the most annoying. I picked this up years ago and have been winding people up with it ever since. Still, it makes a valid point, even though if we followed it religiously we'd probably never utter another word. Here goes.

Before you speak, THINK. Is it

True
Helpful
Inspiring
Necessary
Kind?

If it's not all of those things, shut your mouth.

Done the right way, it can be a liberating experience to hear caring words of guidance from a friend. It can bless us and strengthen our relationship with each other. I know my friends will tell me when something hasn't gone right, and so when they affirm me and tell me that something was good, I am even more inclined to believe what they say. I know they're not just being nice for the sake of it, because I know they would tell me if I'd done a bad talk or if I was out of order. These relationships help me to grow, which is what friendship, and ultimately the Church, should always be aiming for.

Lean on me

These days friendship is hard to find. Those real, true, long-lasting friendships seem to be fading into the past like bad fashion. The modern relationship has taken on the spirit of the age: consumerism. We treat friendships little better than a BHS jumper; at even the slightest sign of a flaw we take it back and demand the perfect product. Once it has worn thin with age, we simply head off and buy a replacement. The tragedy is that some people seem to have closer friendships with their net-friends from the other side of the world, that they meet through the chat rooms and news groups, than they do with those people living in the same time zone. As the Church we need to work on our friendships, we need to work on expressing the love of God with one another, and when we do, our actions will speak loudly to others.

Jazz and the great commandment

It can seem confusing why Jesus decided to add this loving one another commandment just before he died. Wouldn't it have been more sensible to introduce it a little earlier on in the campaign, give it a little more air-time? Perhaps it has the maximum power possible in the present form; Jesus tells the disciples to love as he has loved, and follows up with the most dramatic display of love the world has ever seen. Like any parent, it gives God great pleasure when his children get on – and so true friendship becomes part of our worship. John says in his first letter that if we say we love God but hate our brother, we are liars and the truth is not in us. Those are strong words, but loving God must spill over into loving others, both those who are within the Church and those who aren't.

Another reason that Jesus gave the new commandment was because it was the issue on which he wanted the world to judge us. 'By this shall all men know that you are my disciples, if you have love for one another.' There have been many examples of Christians hating each other, and each one has brought forth an army of critics. By Jesus' own words, their claims are justified. People look at our lives, not just our words. When a loving, caring society is what is on show, it might not provoke quite as much noise but something about it draws people in, intrigued and wanting to know more.

As a teenager, I whiled away many a night in my room,

nodding and tapping to the jazz sounds of Shorty Rogers And His Orchestra Featuring The Giants as they swung their way through a fired-up rendition of that Allen–Adler classic, 'Everybody Loves A Lover'. Old Shorty certainly knew a thing or two about jazz, and the title touched on a truth that we can all relate to; we do love lovers. More importantly, though, God loves lovers; we are meant to be lovers of God, and (in the best way possible) lovers of each other. That's a definition of family, and is where healing comes to the Church. I know that I have received much healing through brothers and sisters who have stood by me through thick and thin. One of the joys I have at Soul Survivor is that the people I work with have been my friends for over ten years. We've seen the worst of each other, we've fallen out loads, yet we're still together. That length of time gives us a security and an honesty that can heal and support in ways that once seemed impossible. God has spoken to me about his commitment to me through the commitment of others to me. In return I want to love others in the way that Jesus loves me.

Live it!

Be vulnerable. Be forgiving. Be a servant. Be honest. You've got to be joking, right? I mean, who can seriously attempt all of those and still maintain a grasp on reality? Surely it's too much to expect?

Friendship is – if you'll pardon the analogy – rather like going to the toilet: we all do it, we all need it, but we don't talk about it that much and we hardly ever pull it apart and really work hard at analysing the components. Get the picture? Thought you might. You see, we're so bad at analysing the way it works (friendship that is) that we end

up believing that in some way it's of diminished importance. But no, for his people friendship is one of God's
commandments and rights. Miraculously we can be friends
with him and we must express that same friendship to
others.

Of course, this has an impact on more than just who we
go to the cinema with. Getting hold of a fully God-focused
vision of friendship in our lives will have some powerful
consequences – not least if there are more than a few of us
doing it. Look, if you will, at the last bit of Acts 2 (from
verse 42 onwards). There you'll see what happened when a
bunch of God-loving people discovered what true friendship meant. Their lives hit the four characteristics we kicked
off with and the rest is, as they say, history. Fancy a bit of
that for yourself?

Task 1

Too many Christians have too few non-church friends. It's
a fact – a sad fact – but a fact nevertheless. There's not the
time to go searching for answers right now, but take time
to look at your own life. Are you shining light, living the
Christian life in view of those who need to see it or are you
locked away in a cosy, holy clique? We're not looking for
quantity here, just quality, so ask God to show you where
you can show some of his inspired friendship to someone
who he'd like to have get to know him better.

Task 2

In the days of the early Church, members were committed
to rooting out factions and ill-feeling whenever it cropped
up. Are there people around with whom things have got a

little sour for you? Do you need to put things right between you, them and God? Ask for strength, grace, humility and tact to repair the damage and seize the next appropriate opportunity.

Task 3

When we ask ourselves how our friendship with God is going, the answer can sometimes be a shock. Find ways of making more time to spend with this most special of friends. Enjoy his company and allow his influence to be shown by the way you live your life.

8
I am a five-cow woman

(a chapter about self-image)

The story

I once heard a student being interviewed on Radio One about what he did in his gap year between school and university. He spent his time travelling around the world, soaking up the experiences that life offered him. When I was at school people didn't take a whole year off; they spent three months in Scotland.

This traveller was telling the DJ about his first destination, which was Indonesia. If I hadn't been so petrified of flying I would have grown increasingly jealous as his description covered the remote islands with white sands and turquoise seas. He wanted to get as involved in the culture as possible, so he travelled to the most remote island he could find.

On the boat trip to the island he noticed a group of locals laughing hysterically. Through an interpreter he asked them what was going on. On this particular island – and I make no comment about it – they had a custom that a woman's hand in marriage was paid for by the groom in cows. There had been no inflation for centuries, and the going rate for an average one would set you back about two and a half moomoos. The most that had ever been paid was five cows, for the most beautiful and perfect woman the island had ever seen. The least was half a cow, which was for one with bits dropping off who was well past her sell-by date. The islanders were all laughing because there was one man who had actually paid five cows for a wife who, at a real push, could only ever be considered a three cow-er. He had been well and truly conned by her father and they all found it particularly funny.

Once the student was on the island, he made up his mind to find the man with such poor bartering skills and let him know what people were saying. Eventually the two met, and our friend from North Devon tactfully told the man that he was a fool with no concept of what a good woman was worth. 'Ah yes,' was the reply, 'I paid for my wife what I wanted to pay for her, and I paid what I thought she was worth. To me she is worth every udder, and when she walks through the village now she walks with her head held high.

She says to herself, "I am a five-cow woman." Because she believes that she is worth five cows, she acts as if she is worth five cows, and she even looks as if she is worth five cows.'

Many of us struggle because we don't know how much we are worth – many of us think our worth doesn't even get near half a cow, but hovers around the half-pint-of-semi-skimmed mark. Instead of opting for Jesus to value us, we estimate our value ourselves. Some of us work it out by the amount of money we have, some of us go by our looks, others by our jobs or friends. If we measure our worth by these values we're in trouble. The good news of the gospel is that God has shown, through the death of his Son on the cross, exactly how much we are worth to him.

The reason why the rates of suicide, anorexia, bulimia and depression have shot up is because we are a generation of people who do not know our worth. We ride an emotional see-saw; at one end we are the sons and daughters of the King of kings, and at the other we are the products of a broken and fallen world. Somewhere in the middle there is a balance, but all too often we are weighed down and broken.

The Conversation

What with me and the co-writer being male, we thought we should get a female perspective in on it, so here comes Emily, a friend from our church. Emily holds a Certificate in Counselling and works with children who've experienced trauma.

  Mike Pilavachi: I reckon one of the main problems we face today is that we don't think we're worth very much. What do you think?

  Emily Barnet: I think that the creation story shows that from the moment we humans sinned, we became insecure. As Adam and Eve stood naked and vulnerable they felt the urge to cover up and hide. From that day on humanity has done the same thing, hiding our real selves and putting up defences. I suppose that because we are no longer in a perfect relationship with God, we don't feel safe and we feel the need to protect ourselves. There are lots of things we hide behind, like being 'the funny one', 'the quiet one' or becoming aggressive.

MP: It might be hard to believe, but I was the funny kid at school. I'd tell jokes and act the fool just to get people to like me. It was the exact opposite of what I was really like; at school I would be Mr Funny, but I'd get home and I'd cry.

EB: I've seen that where I work; children whose behaviour is really difficult will burst into tears and tell all their problems as soon as they are alone. The worst-behaved child in the group once said he wanted to kill himself; he was eight years old. I know that there's a bit of me that thinks nobody would like the real me, so I apologise a lot before someone gets the chance to criticise.

MP: I know someone who so wants to be loved that they take on everybody's pain, and they are always 'the rescuer'. They will always put themselves in a place where they are needed, and at first you think that they are an amazing person, so helpful and considerate. But the truth is that they couldn't cope if they weren't needed. They do good things, but out of bad feelings.

EB: I don't think that the need to be needed always helps the other person.

MP: Yeah, it makes them dependent.

EB: The reason they are being helped isn't that the helper wants them to get better, they are being helped because it's the helper who wants to feel better. If they ever did get sorted, the helper wouldn't be needed. I think that sometimes the helper will keep the other person a few steps away from sorting things out just so that they aren't left alone, without anyone's problems to solve.

MP: There's quite a bit of talk these days about the Twentieth-Century Disorders: anorexia, bulimia, teenage suicide. Even though it's dangerous to generalise, what's your take on them?

EB: When I was at college we talked about each of those things as being a way of 'acting out' very strong feelings. Say you were brought up in a family where there was a lot of violence and anger, you might decide that anger is bad and vow not to express it. That's your defence, but it won't work because to feel angry is human; we all do it, and we all need it. So what do you do when you have an angry feeling? You suppress it, but the feelings have to come out somewhere, and that might be through drinking, depression, anorexia or whatever. Often an anorexic will say that they feel out of control, and so although their life is full of pain they can make themselves feel better by controlling something manageable – their eating. Going without food may make them feel better superficially, but it ignores the real struggles within. The person who suffers from bulimia might feel worthless and empty inside but have no way of expressing it. Bingeing might be a comfort, but then come the feelings of guilt, which also can't be expressed, so the only way of dealing with that is to make yourself sick.

MP: That makes a circle; you feel bad, then you feel

better for a short while, but then you're back where you started.

EB: In a way, I think that you *can* generalise about acting out. Even violence is a way of getting rid of anger, but without expressing it verbally, without confronting it and dealing with it.

MP: Being sexually promiscuous can be part of it, too. Some may just like sleeping around, but I remember one girl who came to a local event our church put on, who was so sexually charged that she did nothing but flirt with the guys. The way she teased them baffled me, and I had no idea why she did it. She then started coming to our celebrations, where she would cry. She told me that when she was younger she was sexually abused by someone in her family. She needed to know that she had power over men because they had caused so much pain in her own life. She was absolutely petrified of getting too close, which made her even more confused: she would sleep around, but she couldn't get close emotionally. When she met Jesus she began to sort things out.

EB: How can meeting Jesus sort things out?

MP: Well, this girl is a good example. During the worship she would cry, even though she didn't have a clue why. I remember her saying that things hurt too much for her to cope. Alcohol was a way out, and she would get drunk to counterbalance the pain. She reminded me of the film *Educating Rita*, where one character tries to commit suicide. Rita asks her why, when she had everything. Trish tells her that when the highs of her life faded, she was left with herself, 'and that's not enough'. With this girl at church, the sex was a cover-up too. In the end Jesus made her face up to the real issues and the pain. We asked her if she wanted to ask Jesus into her life and she said that she was scared, that she had promised herself years before that she would never trust another man again. In asking him in, she had to break her vow. It hasn't been plain sailing, but her life has been so much better for it.

EB: As you say, she had made a promise, and we often tell ourselves things over and over again that are very unhelpful. This can be difficult when we look to Jesus for healing because we are the aspirin generation; we want it all made better right here, right now. Often Jesus does break in and perform a miraculous healing on the spot, but we also have a responsibility to work on things ourselves. If something is so deep-rooted, if it has affected so much of our lives, it may take us a while to learn to live differently, to live better.

MP: We've seen people at Soul Survivor in the summer who have come with such great emotional damage that you wonder how they could ever be healed. But Jesus seems to do it, he loves to heal – and like with everything else covered in the book, we need to find the balance between taking responsibility for our own lives and allowing God time and space to work on us.

EB: We mustn't deny the place of the instant and the miraculous healing, but we must also not ignore the role of the Church in being a place where we can get long-term support and fellowship.

MP: I know that there have been specific times in my life when I've received emotional healing. The first John Wimber conference in 1981 had me down the front as what felt like waves of love washed over me, and at the time something fantastic happened.

There have been other times like that, but I also know that if I didn't have friends around me, like I have for ten years – people who have seen the worst of me but who have stayed with me – I would be walking with a much worse limp than the one I have now.

EB: It can be powerful when we treat someone like they've never been treated before. That's what Jesus did; he called Zaccheus down from the tree and ate with him – nobody ever did that for Zaccheus. By valuing and spending time with each of the disciples I'm sure Jesus laid a vital foundation.

MP: Bearing in mind that everything that Jesus did was of value, what was more significant: feeding the five thousand with five buns and two sardines one afternoon, or living with twelve disciples for three years? Who were the heroes in the Acts of the Apostles? We may never know what happened to the five thousand, but it's pretty clear what Jesus' friendship resulted in with those he was closest to. Both are good – the miraculous and the consistent – but it is important that Jesus did both.

I love the story of the woman caught in adultery. He didn't say to her, 'I accept you as you are, your lifestyle's not that bad.' He looked up from the ground, where he was writing in the dirt, and told anyone who thought they were without sin to throw the first stone. When they had all gone he told her to go and sin no more.

Someone once said to me that they found more acceptance in a pub than in a church. To the degree that statement is true, it's a tragedy. Our job is not to condemn – it doesn't mean compromising on sin, but we are not here to do God's job.

There was the Samaritan woman at the well who

Jesus treated with great dignity even though there were three things wrong with her: she was a Samaritan, she was a sinner (she'd had five husbands and the one she was with was not her husband), and she was a woman (the boys in their Bar Mitzvah would pray this prayer: 'Lord God, I thank you that you have not made me a Gentile. Lord God, I thank you that you have not made me a slave. Lord God, I thank you, oh how I thank you, that you have not made me a woman.'). In that cultural context Jesus treated her with dignity and respect. There can be real healing in something as simple as that.

As well as anorexia and bulimia, I have many friends who have suffered from panic attacks. They range from fear of death to trains, sex or work.

EB: I didn't know much about it until it happened to me. I'd had a very secure upbringing, and couldn't point to any one time where I felt things were terrible. I went off to medical school full of confidence, but really struggled once I got there. Partly things were difficult because I was away from the things that were secure in my life, but mostly it was because I began to realise what drove and motivated me, and that was other people's expectations. I was a 'sorry' person, constantly apologising, believing the way to get by was to get approval from people, and that meant doing whatever they expected. While there wasn't one person who was setting these standards, I think I was making myself reach for the sky.

The work at college was harder and more frequent than any I had experienced before and it didn't take long before I felt completely out of my depth. During my exams at the end of the first term I first had the panic attacks. I remember waking up in the night, petrified that I was going to fall out of the window. They were so intense that I often would go and get a friend to sit with me – I wouldn't really tell them what was going on – until I calmed down. The attacks came more often, and at the start of the summer I told my parents that I was going to leave college – something in me knew the two things were related.

Over the summer I calmed down and went back in September. Immediately the panic attacks returned and I was gripped with this fear of letting people down and being a disappointment to everyone. I started getting afraid of all sorts of things: being on my own, going on trains, being around knives. Eventually I phoned my vicar, and he totally shocked me by telling me that I didn't have to be at college. I had been working under the belief that being at college was exactly what I did need to be doing – how else was I going to please people? That was a real turning point, and he sent me off to have a chat with one of the doctors in the church. I told him all about my fears, and was kind of prepared for him to pack me off to the psychiatric ward. Instead, he said that my head was like a pressure cooker – there were all these expectations on me but no way of letting the steam out. He told me that a panic attack does just that, releases the stress when it has all got too much. Unless you deal with the cause of the anxiety, you are bound to have irrational fears. I thought that I was dealing with my fears by giving in to them, but really I was letting them take over and control my life.

That day was an amazing day – I felt an amazing sense of freedom at the end of it – but it then took months for me to start looking at the roots of what had caused the problems in the first place. I had missed the point about what I was worth. I thought that my work was the only way that I was going to get God's approval.

Sometimes we can read a chapter like this and think that it's fine for others to look inside themselves and understand what's going on, but as for us, we don't know how we feel, we don't even know if we feel anything at all. It's a common enough problem, particularly among young men. They have been brought up with male role models who have the old stiff upper lip.

MP: And, you know, I'm worried that it will only be the girls that read this chapter. We have somehow come to a point where men think they don't need to express themselves, and I think that's very dangerous. We need to encourage young men to believe that it's OK to look in on the 'feminine side', that it's OK to feel things deeply.

EB: Haven't we seen this at church, where the girls find it so much easier to make relationships than the boys . . . ?

MP: But when the guys do make strong and supportive friendships it's fantastic.

EB: I wonder whether we know what it is to be a man these days. Back in the fifties – however good or bad it was – the man had a clearly defined role as the breadwinner, with an established position in society. Today we have more and more women in the workplace – which is a fantastic thing – but more and more men are wondering what use they are. In no way am I suggesting that locking women up in the kitchen will bring the male suicide rate down, but I think we have a responsibility to be aware of the climate and be ready to understand how men feel these days.

MP: I don't think that women competing with men for jobs is wrong either, but I do think that some of the more intense girl-power stuff is actually belittling to men. Men and women are different, that's where the attraction lies, but when the differences are ignored it gets tough.

The answer to all of this is first to discover what God thinks of us, that our value is more than just sixteen stone of flesh and bone, that we are worth more than two and a half cows. God says, if you want to know how much you are worth, look at the cross; I went out and bought you, and I paid the price of my Son. It can be hard to accept his valuation. When you've always believed that you're worth nothing it's a heck of a job to believe that you're worth the life of Jesus. That's why we need to discover more of God through worship and through our friendships – go back and read the Loving One Another chapter. As the second commandment is to love our neighbour as we love ourselves, you can't truly love your neighbour unless you know your own worth.

EB: Sometimes the solution really is that practical; we need to find those verses that say how much we are worth, we need to find someone who can pray things through with us. It isn't always that easy, though; some people are in a church where there doesn't seem to be anyone to turn to.

MP: Yes, that's hard, but it's so important. There might be someone from another church or at school or college, but as long as they can be trusted sometimes all it takes is having someone who is willing to listen and then pray things through. They don't need to be a wonderful prophet or preacher, just find someone who will be there. I'm not saying that working through any of this stuff is easy, but it is so worth the effort. Ultimately living the life is all about becoming more like Jesus, giving God the chance to restore us to the people he intended us to be.

Live it!

It was a few years ago that *Live the Life* was written, and while very little has changed – I still feel the same about things (including chocolate) – the issues surrounding self-image have shifted the most. It seems that things are more intense these days, and the rate of self-image related problems that crop up in churches has increased. Maybe it's just an opinion, but it seems to me that we are even more unsure of who we're supposed to be, we're even more desperate to be thin in order to be loved and we're even less certain of what the future will hold.

So where does Christianity come into all this? What does Jesus have to say about cellulite, six-packs and twenty-first-century masculinity and femininity? There's no magic formula to get us back on the right track, and in a way, we've been continually struggling with the consequences of Adam and Eve's scrumpying in the Garden of Eden. We're living with the consequences of a back turned on God, and until we are one day face to face again, I wonder whether we will ever know what true wholeness feels like. But there is hope, and it comes not in the form of wondering what God can do for us, but in thinking about what we can do for others. It's vital that the church starts pumping out some positive messages about identity and it's essential that we on the ground get down to the business of communicating God's acceptance of all people *no matter what*. Of course let's not deny the fact that we are all broken, let's not stop the journey we're all making towards wholeness, but we must not allow ourselves to become voiceless victims: we've got loads to say so let's get on and say it!

Task 1

Use a Bible concordance to check out references to words like flock, child, precious and shepherd. Build up a picture in your mind of the language the Bible uses to express how God feels about his creation. Are there any verses you come across that surprise you? Try meditating on a different verse each day.

Task 2

Look through the gospels and focus on the way that Jesus treated the various people that he met. Who was he gentle with? Which type of people did he say harsher things to? What did those around him think of the way he treated people? What does the way Jesus behaved towards people tell you about how he feels about you as well as how you might behave towards others?

Task 3

Imagine that you're a fly on the wall of your own mind. Write a letter to God telling him about the secret thoughts and feelings that go on inside you. Once you've written it leave it for a few days. Then, read it again and have a go at

writing God's reply, asking him to inspire you with the
words that express how he feels about you.

9

Learning to catch

(a chapter about healing)

God wants more than anything to have his children turn back to him. But it doesn't stop there; once we start working on our relationship with him, allowing bits of his nature to rub off on us, we notice that the gap between our broken-ness and his perfection begins, ever so slightly, to narrow. In short, we begin to get healed. Part of being the friend of God is to take up his offers of healing as, like a parent with a baby, he steadies us on our feet, getting us ready to walk. True, we are never going to be sorted this side of heaven, but turning him down is not an option. God has both the power and the desire to heal us – not just our skin and bone, but our hearts and minds too. As we learn to lean on him more, we tap into a source of incredible power.

Jesus knew that he was on the earth for a purpose. Just after we read about his baptism in the Holy Spirit, we hear what happened when he went into his local synagogue one Sabbath. He stood up to read and was handed the scroll of the prophet Isaiah. Unrolling it, he found the place where it is written:

> The Spirit of the Lord is on me,
>> because he has anointed me to preach good news to
>> the poor.
> He has sent me to proclaim freedom for the prisoners
> and recovery of sight for the blind,
> to release the oppressed,
>> to proclaim the year of the Lord's favour.
>> (Luke 4:18–19)

Then he rolled up the scroll, gave it back to the attendant and sat down. Every eye was fixed on him. Was the son of a carpenter seriously claiming that he was the Great Hope for the whole nation? Then came Jesus' answer: 'Today this scripture is fulfilled in your hearing.'

What Jesus showed

Through his life Jesus showed the importance of relying on the Holy Spirit, as well as the effectiveness of praying for healing. After he was thrown out of Nazareth, we follow his life through the gospels and we see that he was right to read this passage from Isaiah; the Spirit of the Lord *was* on him, and he *did* have the power. He preached good news to the prostitutes and to the tax collectors, to the publicans and the sinners. He spent time with the outcasts, telling and encouraging them that one day they would be first in the kingdom of heaven. He gave blind people back their sight. Some were physically blind, and others were spiritually blind. Those who had been prisoners of their emotions could once again feel the sun on their faces.

Jesus came down to earth and brought with him the biggest goody bag ever seen. Regardless of whether people had earned or deserved his blessings, he travelled around and spread the healing good and thick. Jesus had such compassion, such love for the people, that he couldn't help himself; to heal was the most natural thing in the world for him.

The fact that the area was bursting with cripples who could walk, blind who could see and lepers who were clean again was a sign that the kingdom of God was real and accessible. Hearing of all those miracles opened people's eyes, and the word spread. As well as showing God's love, healing people showed that God was alive.

The healing didn't stop when Jesus left us. He told the disciples that they were to watch out for the Holy Spirit who would guide and comfort them, helping them take the message out to the rest of the world. At Pentecost the Spirit showed up and made quite an impression. The disciples went on to lay down the law with their preaching, and did good deeds and works by healing the sick, casting out demons and raising the dead. The life they lived was modelled on what they had seen while Jesus was on the earth.

One day Peter and John were going up to the temple at the time of prayer – at three in the afternoon. Now a man crippled from birth was being carried to the temple gate called Beautiful, where he was put every day to beg from those going into the temple courts. When he saw Peter and John about to enter, he asked them for money. Peter looked straight at him, as did John. Then Peter said, 'Look at us!' So the man gave them his attention, expecting to get something from them.

Then Peter said, 'Silver or gold I do not have, but what I have I give you. In the name of Jesus Christ of Nazareth, walk.' Taking him by the right hand, he helped him up, and instantly the man's feet and ankles became strong. He jumped to his feet and began to walk. Then he went with them into the temple courts, walking and jumping, and praising God. When all the people saw him walking and praising God, they recognised him as the same man who used to sit begging at the temple gate called Beautiful, and they were filled with wonder and amazement at what had happened to him.

(Acts 3:1–10)

The good stuff didn't die with the early Christians either. Today we have just as much of a job to do as they did, sharing the same tools. The Bible is more than a history book. The apostles took the stories of how Jesus went about his business as blueprints for their own behaviour, and it is still the same for us today. Our friends and society need to know that God is alive and loving, and, should we choose to accept it, we can set out on our mission fully equipped. The Spirit of the Lord is still here with his people, the Church, still setting the captives free and binding up the broken-hearted. Today God is saying to his people, 'I want to use all of you to do my work.'

Early days

I was in a bit of a state when I arrived at St Andrew's Chorleywood. I was bruised and hurt, tired of feeling like a featherweight sparring partner for some particularly vicious heavyweights. I used to sit at the back of the church, soaking up the vibes as God mingled with his people. At the end of each service there were opportunities for people who wanted prayer to go up to the front and have members of the ministry team pray for them. At first I just watched, checking to see which team members were consistently getting results in the healing department. I watched the people who were being prayed for and worked out that, on the whole, good things seemed to happen. Often at the start of the following week's service people would stand up and say what had happened to them, and how God had worked in them.

Having devised a particularly elaborate scoring system (based on numbers of falling-overs, weepings, shakings and shoutings) I decided which team member was a pro and headed for him at the end of one particular service. This was a busy evening up the front, and in the confusion my pro-prayer got nabbed by a woman with swollen ankles. I was left with a second-division team member – not quite what I'd hoped for, but I felt generous so I let him carry on. That night I met God and was filled by his Spirit. Something happened in me, something was re-ignited.

After that I went up for prayer regularly, until I panicked that people might start to think that I was one of those sort of people who were always going up for prayer. Then after one service the vicar stopped me as I was leaving. There was no way of escape, so I decided to face up to the inevitable charge of being One Of Those Sort Of People . . . To my surprise he didn't give me a slap, but asked me to join the ministry team myself. I said yes before he could find out that I was as unspiritual as a hole-punch and change his mind.

At the beginning I was put with someone who was more experienced and who knew what to say. I acted as the assistant, and worked out that, if nothing else, I could at least have a go at catching people if they fell down. Soon I had become expert in a number of radical techniques, not least The Sidewinder, The Back Flip and The Double Whammy.

I saw God minister to people when we prayed, but deep down I really thought that it was because of the other person's prayers and not mine. At times I would feel down, but it all changed in an instant.

It was mid-June, and a number of visitors had turned up at the church. So many people came forward that I had to pray with someone on my own. A sudden terror hit me. I pleaded with God to give me someone with a mild headache, but instead I ended up with a bloke in his thirties. I asked him what his problem was.

'Well, there's two things. I've had a problem in my lower back for a number of years, and I've also been suffering from depression. That's it, really.'

My mind crashed: panic . . . fear . . . help . . . run away . . . lie. 'Let's have a bash at the depression, shall we?' I said, after a few minutes had passed. I prayed the first thing that came into my head: 'Lord, please would you come and heal his depression.' I waited (because that's what they told us to do), and was trying to work out some decent excuses for why he would still feel depressed when he opened his eyes and said, 'That was amazing. It just feels like it's lifted, I feel like I'm floating on air.'

'Really?!' I said. I could hardly believe it. I thought it might be good to have a go at praying for his back, so I put my hand on his back and asked the Lord to heal that, too. After a while he opened his eyes and thanked me for my

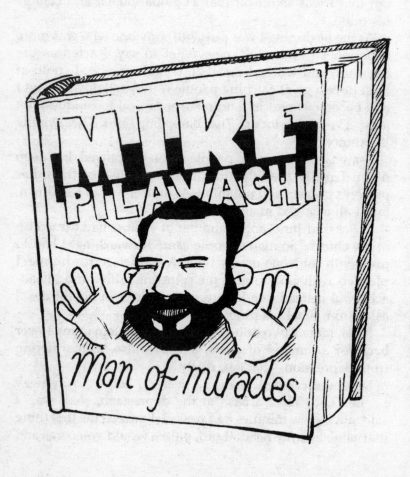

prayers. I figured the back wasn't healed, but a 50 per cent success rate wasn't bad for a beginner.

Soon he came running up to me, jumping about wildly and showing me how his back was completely healed. I left the church walking on air. I knew then that I was holy, spiritual, the possessor of a rare healing ministry. I planned my first book – *Mike Pilavachi, Man of Miracles*. I couldn't wait for the next Sunday to come so I could pray for someone again. Perhaps we should go to the cemetery...

The next Sunday came and I prayed for someone. This time, though, nothing much appeared to happen to them. I prayed harder than ever before but still nothing happened. I was puzzled and asked God why, when I expected nothing, he did so much the week before, but when I was ready to see miracles this week I might as well have been praying to a gnome. A classic verse came into my mind again: 'God opposes the proud but gives grace to the humble.' I realised that I was getting proud and was missing the point of it all. It never was supposed to be about me having a great ministry, or even having a great time. At the end of the day it's all about him, about his generosity, his grace and his ability to heal.

How do you pray for healing?

So, having sussed out that praying for people is a good thing to be doing and having got clear on just how much of an ego trip it should be for us, we come to the nuts and bolts of it and ask how. First, to pray for healing is not to pray a 2,000-word essay on the root causes of society's fall from grace. Nor is it to shout so loud and propel so much saliva into the subject's face that they break down in tears.

Here's what you can do:

1 Ask the person what they want prayer for. At this stage you aren't after a full medical diagnosis

complete with case notes, just a rough idea of what's wrong. If possible, get them to show you what's wrong, because at the end you'll have something to measure against what God has done.

2　Tell them to relax and that you're going to pray for them. It can help them if they have their eyes closed and their hands out in front, as if they were about to receive a present – which, hopefully, is exactly what is going to happen.

3　Invite the Holy Spirit. You can pray something like, 'Lord Jesus, please send your Holy Spirit now.' We do this because we want God to do the healing, and Jesus told us that the Holy Spirit would be more than pretty handy in this sort of situation. Having asked him to come, it's time to wait.

4　After a while you may notice that they start to look more peaceful. Or they might just look the same. Either way, just wait.

5　And wait some more.

6　If we ask he will come, so it's important to wait for as long as it takes. Once they do look more peaceful – or maybe they've started to sway a little – you will want to pray some more. If it's a physical problem you might want to pray something like, 'Lord, I pray that you would heal this . . .' You may feel that it is appropriate to say, 'In the name of Jesus, be healed.' Alternatively you may just want to pray quietly, or gently put your hand on their shoulder or (if it's not too personal) on whatever bit of their body needs healing. This also applies to praying for people's emotions; you can pray out loud if you feel you have something to say, but at the end of the day it's up to God. We're just helping the person to focus on him.

7　Then you need to wait some more. Carry on

asking God to heal them, and thank him if you think something's going on. Even if you're desperate to get home it is vital that the person who has come for prayer leaves feeling loved and valued. That means no laughing at them, talking about their dress sense to your mate or walking off for a coffee halfway through. When they're good and ready they'll open their eyes and you can have a little chat about what they thought was going on.

8 At the end of it all you might want to pray briefly again, thanking God for what he's done and asking him to bless and keep on looking after them. Often things get started in a ministry time but get finished days later, so it can be useful to suggest that they keep on praying too, looking out for God doing things in them.

9 Don't ask for a tip.

Putting on a good show

Of course, what really doesn't matter in all of this is making it look good. As you can tell from my early experiences, trying to force the situation just doesn't work. The whole process may take a long time or it may be over in a flash. The person may jump around or stand completely still. Whatever happens, there is no need to try and make something happen. When we ask the Lord to come, we are asking for a gift from him, not some nonsense that we find floating around in the backwaters of our mind. In Luke 11:9–13 Jesus says that we should 'Ask and it will be given–' So whenever we ask we can leave it all up to him.

Sometimes when we pray for someone to be filled with the Holy Spirit, to hear God's voice for direction or to be healed physically or emotionally, we will see certain things happen. There can sometimes be shaking, sometimes laughter. Sometimes they might lie down on the floor. It won't always be the case, and we don't encourage them, but when these things do happen it's good to see them, like smoke coming out of a chimney. It might be a sign that someone's home, but then again they may have central heating. Either way, it's what's going on inside that really counts. The goal is not the physical manifestation, the goal is that we meet with Jesus and we give him space and time to work on our lives. The goal is that, like Jesus and the apostles who followed him, we let people know that God is both generous and alive.

Respect

We want to treat people with the dignity and respect that all children of God deserve. We have found at Soul Survivor, and at other places, that when we give the Holy Spirit the room to move he often tackles some really deep hurts. As buried pain comes up to the surface, it can often get people weeping. The key to praying for someone in this situation is respect, both for the person – how would you feel if you were them? would it be better if you found somewhere more private to pray? – and for what God is doing – if there's that much emotion, use common sense and realise that God is probably at work. Keep encouraging the person to stick with what God is doing, and keep asking God to do whatever he wants.

How do you begin?

Praying for people alongside the Holy Spirit is like cooking; you can get all the books, listen to all the tapes and watch all the videos, but the only way to really learn is to get on and do it. I found it helped to have someone more experienced to team up with at first. This way, if it's a member of the opposite sex you can pray for anyone. But if you're on your own or with someone of the same sex it's generally a pretty good rule to pray only with someone who has the same 'equipment' as you, otherwise things can get a little complicated.

God created us as well as the universe. Therefore it is obvious that we should ask him to restore the bodies he has made, to heal the hearts that he understands and to fill with his power the lives he created. Because of this it is vital that we don't hype anything up, we just let the Holy Spirit come down. We need to exercise the gift of faith when we pray for others, to trust that God knows what he's doing and will do something good. Because he is God, occasionally some of the ways he does things are hard to understand.

In 1 Corinthians 12 we have a list of some of the gifts of the Spirit – one of them is 'the gift of healing'. Who gets the gift of healing? Surprisingly, it is not the person doing the praying but the person who needs the healing. There is no such thing as a group of people who carry the gift of healing around in their pockets. None of us is so spiritual that we carry that gift with us wherever we go. Instead, we need to see ourselves as waiters and waitresses in a restaurant. When we pray for someone we take their order and pass it on to the chef. Only he can prepare the dish. We get to have the fun of being involved in delivering the dish to the diner. Healing is something God does, not us.

Why bother?

None of this is meant so that we can have a cosy life, sitting around on those long winter nights, adding the finishing touches to our near-perfect souls. As we learn to pray for one another in these ways in the Church, God is preparing us to pray for people out in the world. Most of the miraculous healings and deliverances that happened in the New Testament, both in the life of Jesus and in the early Church, happened outside the synagogue. Instead of setting up an exclusive service for members only, Jesus took it out to the people. Let's practise in the Church but not forget to take it with us when we go out.

This might be making you feel uncomfortable. The idea of inviting people up to the front of the bus for deliverance might not quite be your cup of tea. Truth is, it's not mine either. What we can do is learn to pray for people in a normal way, without the jargon and religion. Praying for someone who knows nothing of God or Church has a maximum risk factor and, because of that, a massive potential for God to do something great. Let's devote ourselves to learning how to pray for people outside the safety of the Church, just like Jesus did.

Many Christians think of the Holy Spirit as an 'it'. He is not an 'it', he is a 'he'. When we think of God the Father, we understand the concept because most of us have had fathers (however good or bad they are). When we think of Jesus we imagine a person, whether we picture him with long blond hair and a white nightie or (as in the *Jesus of Nazareth* film) with long black hair and a brown nightie. The Holy Spirit is much harder to visualise, but he is full of personality. The early Church all knew that the Holy Spirit was for real and trusted him to do his thing. Knowing this will encourage us to trust in his power and not just our own.

Live it!

How else can a chapter like this have an impact on our daily lives? It seems that many of the models for healing and praying for people that we're given during sermons at church are only really suitable for use within church. I mean, you try asking some atheist with a viral infection to 'relax and let yourself open up to God' while they're standing in the middle of a crowded shopping centre. Not the easiest of tasks, am I right?

So does this mean that God's gift of healing is only for use down the front of church after the meeting? Is it only available to those who are already signed up? Does it lose its power the minute we leave the vestry? One look at the New Testament and the answer 'no' is heard loud and clear: Jesus and his disciples, followed by the members of the early Church, were well into using heavenly gifts in whatever setting needed them most. When Peter and John bumped into the crippled beggar outside the temple gate they didn't drag him inside to perform the necessary. No; they did it right there, right then. The same is true of Jesus when he was confronted by the young man who continually slashed himself with rocks. Did Jesus suggest that they reconvene at a later date when he was in a better frame of mind? No way, and before we know it there's one happy lad and one drowned herd of pigs. Simple as that.

But still we struggle, still we seem to be locked into this idea that God's gifts are best used in God's house. Why? Well, it's obviously potentially horrifically embarrassing to do the holy biz in public, but is it really wise to be saying such a 'no' to God? I mean, isn't it just a tad on the rude side? As you decide to step out bear this in mind: God is already at work all around us and it's not us who are doing the miracles, it's him.

Task

Think of people around you who need to know God's healing touch – they might be physically ill or they might be struggling with something else that's stressing them out. Make a list of four or five and commit yourself to praying for them every day. Experiment with different ways of praying for them too: from taking their problems to God in your mind to using music, candles and whatever else helps, perhaps being a bit more vocal about it. Ask the Holy Spirit to provide opportunities for you to say something, to offer to pray. Don't be surprised by when or where the opportunities arise; just concentrate on being a faithful servant of God, leaving the miracles fully in his capable hands. Then what? Why, keep on praying of course.

Also, there is the saying 'The meeting place is the learning place for the market place.' Decide to use every opportunity that arises to pray for healing. If any of your Christian friends are sick, offer to pray for them. Make praying for healing a natural part of your life, lay hands on those who are not well, watch, pray and wait.

Part III
Go

10

Why I left Harrow

(a chapter about evangelism)

I want you to come on a journey with me. We are headed
for North London in the mid-seventies. Big-haired rock is
just about to give birth to a difficult baby named Punk, but

our hero (me) remains completely oblivious to the noise. Instead my 'mono' is banging out the sounds of the Carpenters, Simon and Garfunkel and Max Bygraves' Christmas Favourites (there weren't many record shops round our way). Society is going through a tough period; marriage doesn't seem to be worth much, what is important is the business of enjoying your own life, making sure you have a good time. As I seemed to be the only teenage Christian in the Borough of Harrow and Wealdstone it made perfect sense that I appoint myself Last Hope For The Lost People Round Here. Slim, tanned and enthusiastic, I was ready to take on the world, one postal district at a time. I spent weeks planning the offensive that would bring my neighbours to their knees. It was only a matter of a few days' hard work and people would be throwing themselves at my feet as I walked to the garage, begging me to make personal introductions between them and God. I had found my weapon in a little-known bookshop; small, round and to the point, it was all perfectly simple – stickers.

At the time Coca-Cola was forcing its way into the population's subconscious with the slogan 'Coke – it's the real thing'. The stickers were an exact copy, except for the fact that the word 'Coke' was replaced by the name 'Jesus'. Perhaps the manufacturers had been in a rush, as they seemed to have forgotten to change the 'it's' to 'he's', which meant they were a bit confusing, but I was sure that people would get the idea. I bought all they had and spent the next two nights applying them to every available surface: lamp-posts, cars, shop windows, coin slots on collection boxes, even the occasional dog. By the end I had stuck up 743 of them. I sat back and waited for the revival to break. If each sticker was seen by twenty people per day I was sure that by tea-time the streets would be full of people weeping and wailing, ready for the short sermon I had prepared.

It was a week later that I returned to the Christian bookshop. Nobody had approached me directly since my sticker campaign, although a couple of dogs did seem to be hanging around my house a bit more than usual. I was just about to ask the assistant for some more supplies when I heard her tell another customer about a particular problem she was encountering. I moved closer.

'It's terrible – we've had so many calls from people who are totally irate about these stickers. It's such a bad witness and I've been going round scraping them off wherever I can.'

I left the shop.

The best way to evangelise

Christians have been arguing for years about the best way to evangelise. A whole bunch (let's call them 'conservative evangelicals') have said that the way to do it is to preach it. For them, nothing else quite cuts the mustard as getting up and proclaiming the good news with a clear voice. They point to Jesus as an example of preaching leading to conversions, and take Paul's trips as proof that hearing the word is the most sure way of someone becoming a Christian.

We have another group in the Church (we might call them the 'social gospellers') who say that the thing that counts is the way we live – that the gospel is best preached through our deeds. They say that people are tired of words, what they want is action. The gospels, they say, are full of references to what Jesus did as well as to what he said, and it is the things he did that caught people's attention. These people say that the gospel that is waiting to be heard is actually a gospel that can be seen – a gospel that makes a difference to people's lives. We've got to build people houses, care for the Third World, get involved in ecology and so on. They quote Francis of Assisi, who said to his followers, 'Go into all the world and preach the gospel – if necessary, use words.'

What really matters to the third group, (the 'charismatics') are signs and wonders – this is the idea that when people see they believe. They point to the Scriptures and say that what actually caught people's attention were the miracles, the supernatural things. When Jesus healed, people listened; when he prophesied, they were all ears. Today, say the charismatics, people want to see, feel and touch the power of God, not just to hear about it.

Which one of these three is the right opinion? The answer, I believe, is all of them; the way to get the gospel out on to the streets is through a combination of each of the three.

Jesus gave us a gospel to proclaim through words, works and wonders, and when we miss out one or two of them the power of the gospel is never as strong. Jesus proclaimed the gospel in the things he said. If we don't say, people won't know. He also lived it in the way he cared for people, in the way he sided with the marginalised – he spent time with the publicans and the sinners and the prostitutes and the tax collectors and those rejected by polite society. He had a ministry of power, he did miracles, he healed and changed lives. In the Acts of the Apostles, we see the same thing, the three ingredients of communicating the gospel coming together to make one big evangelism pie. We might like a little more of one taste than another, but the pie just won't be a pie unless we have each ingredient represented. The trouble with my Sticker Ministry was that it contained none of the above; as a pie, it sucked.

Early experiences in Watford

In between the stickers and today there have been plenty of mistakes, but by 1993, when eleven of us decided to set up a new church in Watford, we had got through the worst of it. When we started Soul Survivor Watford we all met in someone's front room. Looking around at the other ten I panicked, totally unconvinced that God could do anything at all through them (as for myself, well, I knew what ground-breaking foul-ups I was capable of). We found that in the early days the thing that we needed to concentrate on was not the preaching of the gospel with words or even through signs and wonders, but through the work of making friendships. Why should people be bothered to hear what we had to say if they didn't know us?

Soon after we started two fourteen-year-old lads turned up, both with long greasy hair and questionable personal hygiene – they were a nightmare. Dave had been thrown out of his house by his parents because he'd tried to set fire to it. Social Services had placed him with a Christian family whose sons had started coming to our little church. Dave and Liam were into everything that we weren't – drugs, drink, fighting – and I was convinced that it was the very worst state of affairs for us to be in.

Both lads started coming to our social meetings first of all. One of the early turning points was when we had an evening in with a curry and a video. Dave challenged me to a vindaloo-eating competition, and I have never consciously turned down a food-related challenge. I nearly died and he beat me hands down. He was so chuffed that I decided not to ask him to leave, and actually, it was this sort of thing that helped us all become good friends.

As well as eating, we used to meet to worship, pray and listen to God. I remember one Wednesday evening looking around as everybody was deep in worship, and Dave had disappeared from sight. I guessed that he had finally got bored by it all, but I went to look for him just in case. I found him sitting on the floor behind the sofa with his head down. He was crying, and I asked what was wrong. 'All this stuff about Jesus,' he said, 'it's really true, isn't it?' He gave his life to Jesus there and then, but none of this would have happened if he hadn't grown to trust and like us.

We Christians have a phrase that we quite like, that Jesus is the answer. There are plenty of non-Christians out there who quite rightly reply, 'But what's the question?' We are trying to give answers to questions that aren't even being asked. It ought to be a natural by-product of our friendship with people who don't know Jesus that they begin to ask about him. It should come from within rather than being forced down their throats by our impatience. Dave, incidentally, is still with us, and we love him and we've seen him grow. He's part of us.

We started an outreach event called Dreggs Café which

aimed to give us an opportunity to make friends with people. This wasn't supposed to be done in a patronising way, but because we genuinely wanted to get on with developing good relationships. We decided that we would never preach at them, and we would only talk about God if they brought the subject up. Mostly we danced, played cards, ate and drank and just had a laugh together. People started coming from the different schools in Watford, and the first thing many of them said was that they liked it because the people were nice.

Over time it was amazing to see lasting friendships develop, and a number of people came to know Jesus because first of all they came to know us. We have this little saying that we've nicked from somewhere (but we can't remember where we've nicked it from), which goes like this: the order is belonging, believing, behaving. Traditionally the Church has said to people that if they want to come along they must behave themselves. A stranger to church must adjust to the way we do church, standing up at the correct times, sitting down when required. What the rest of the congregation read out, the stranger has to read out as well, and they certainly don't snog on the back pew, smoke during the sermon or use the news sheet to make paper aeroplanes. Once the behaviour thing has been sorted out and they can imitate the rest of the church, then they stay long enough to hear the gospel preached and get round to believing. Only once they believe do we baptise them, sing a cheesy little song about how welcome they are and proclaim that they finally belong.

Call me Mr Cynical, but I would suggest that Jesus did it the other way around. When he called the disciples to himself, he called them to belong to him, to be together and be a family. Their believing then came in stages; for some of them to leave their nets and follow Jesus must have meant some kind of belief, but we only have to look at

Thomas to see a man who took his time to believe. Even after three years of Jesus' company he still demanded to see the nail marks in his hands and touch the side of the resurrected Jesus. John 20 verse 9 says that even at the end the disciples still did not understand from Scripture that Jesus had to rise from the dead. Duh!

As for their behaviour, that also took some time to sort out. James and John were nicknamed 'sons of thunder', not because of their high-fibre diets, but due to the fact that they could never control their tempers. Peter was always putting his foot in it; Judas betrayed Jesus. Even in the garden of Gethsemane, when Jesus was in his last hours, out of twelve disciples, one betrayed him, ten ran away and one stayed long enough to tell three lies and then legged it. Great behaviour. The belonging most definitely came first, and was only then followed by the believing, which came a long way before the behaviour even began to get sorted.

We need to make space in the Church for our friends, so that they know they belong. At Soul Survivor Watford it seemed like there were quite a few that found the transition from going to the Dreggs Café to coming along to church wasn't very difficult. They already knew us and we had become friends.

Probably the best evangelism in the world

It seems pretty clear that the best evangelism comes out of friendships because, as the saying goes, 'the only Bible some people will read is you'. But we wanted more than just the friendships, we wanted people to have a chance to meet Jesus. Just relying on preaching the gospel through our works would have left us unsatisfied. By inviting them along to church they had a chance to have it shown them, not only through the words of the talk and the songs, but also through the signs and wonders of a full-on ministry session.

After Dreggs had been going for a while and people were taking us up on our offers of a night out at church, we started to think that the whole system was a pretty good way of showing our new friends that we weren't a group of sad weirdos. Then came Toronto. Suddenly our meetings were interrupted by a repertoire of animal impressions that would have had Old MacDonald calling up for some farm help. God was doing something great in the hearts of his people, but it all seemed to be happening in a very bizarre way. The plan of laying on a little worship followed by a very good talk from a wonderfully well-known preacher leading to their positive responses to the gospel was, I thought, ruined. 'Lord,' I prayed, 'this is wonderful, but not here.' The Lord and I had a bit of a discussion about the whole thing, and at the end we came to an agreement that since he was God and I wasn't, we'd try it his way first. To my amazement the people who found it easiest were the non-Christians, whereas it was some of the Christians who found the weird stuff difficult.

One day five people arrived at church together for the first time. They had been to Dreggs a few times and said that they wanted to come along on a Sunday. Of all the people we had met, I was convinced that these were the ones who were going to leave the minute the service started. I lost sight of them for bit, but found them towards the end of the meeting. Each one was lying face down on the floor. I asked one of the girls what was going on. 'I dunno,' she replied helpfully. Digging a bit deeper, I asked whether it was a good dunno or a bad dunno. She said it was a good one.

'Do you know it's Jesus?' I asked.

'I think so,' she said. I asked her if she had asked him into her life and she hadn't.

'Would you like to do it now?'

'Yes.' So we clinched the deal there and then.

Back down to earth

A couple of weeks later a youth leader friend of mine came up to see how Dreggs was going. To be honest, I was showing off my little trophies, all those new Christians, which was an awful thing to do. We got to one of the five that had wound up on the floor two weeks back, and I asked her to tell Silas the story of how she became a Christian. Becky said that when she turned up at church she was an atheist, going along just to be with her friends. 'Then the Holy Spirit came on me and I fell down.' She obviously needed some help with this testimony thing, so I reminded her that she had missed out the bit about how in the worship she sensed something wonderful. That was then followed by the sermon which explained Christianity so well that she decided to give her life to Jesus, and then the Holy Spirit came and she fell down.

'No,' she interrupted, 'I went down an atheist and came up a Christian.'

In Becky's case the wonders and the works worked very closely together – it was the power of God at work that convinced her, and she wouldn't have come along if she hadn't had friends there – but at the same time there had to be a place for explaining what was happening as well as what the cross meant to her. Words, works and wonders need to exist together; we need to be flexible in our approach to each person, but at the same time make sure that we value each way of expressing the gospel. When we miss out on one we take away from the fullness of the message of the cross.

There have been many studies into the growth of churches which have ended up agreeing on the same point: that we appeal to those people that are most like us. The thing about friendship evangelism is that the friendship needs to be genuine. When Dreggs was going on, I wasn't the first person up leading the moves for Whigfield's Saturday Night, nor was I comparing stunts with the skaters outside. Dreggs attracted people who were like most of the people in our church.

The key to it all is to love people for who they are, not for another notch on your conversions chart. People can sniff a rat without too much trouble. We had to reach a point where we were going to love and care for people whether they made a response or not, but we were never going to hide the fact that we would love them to make a response because we believe that Christianity is a fantastic, life-changing thing.

Reading this might give you an impression that everybody that walked through the doors of the Dreggs Café ended up on their knees at the foot of the cross. Unfortunately that didn't always happen. The majority of people became our friends and left it at that. We had one guy who came all the time but who never made a commitment. While we knew there was more for him in Jesus, we had to leave it to him, happy that friendship is a valid way of expressing God's love. We are called to love people as God loves them, unconditionally. Our primary calling is to care for people – that's where the works of social action come in. We serve the poor because we love God.

We Christians are supposed to be the nicest people around, the most generous with our time and money. Our friendships must be because God calls us to be friends with people, to be good and caring people. We are called to proclaim the gospel with our words and our lives and with the power of God, modelling ourselves on the life of Jesus.

Postscript

As I walked home from the bookshop, feeling sick inside as I remembered the shop assistant's view of my sticker idea, I thought of a new evangelism strategy. I would open the phone book at a random page, pick and dial a number and play some worship down the phone, immediately bringing the listener to their knees. The only trouble was, the closest thing I had to worship music was Max Bygraves' version of 'The Holly and the Ivy'. It was worth a shot.

Live it!

Of course, I left Harrow because it had all got a bit too much, because to some extent I'd messed up and desperately needed a God-given way out. But looking back, I wonder whether it also might have been a thoroughly natural consequence of being reflective about the way we live our lives with God. You see, I don't think there's anything wrong with getting in a complete state and needing God's help. In fact, I think that it's actually rather healthy. To get to the point where we realise that we're unable to carry on in our own strength, to realise that it is God on whom we are 100% dependent, well, that's quite possibly the most ideal place for us Christians to be. And if it's with this in mind that we approach the area of evangelism that we stand the best chance of doing the right thing by God and others. Let's ditch that old idea that says evangelism is all about us arguing people into the kingdom: there's far too much room for the distorted belief that it's something to do with our own abilities. Instead let's get back to basics: evangelism is not about the slickness of our performance but the extent to which we can allow people to see God without us getting in the way. To that extent it's just like worship and our job is to be the faithful servants. Words, works and wonders; that's what we should be aiming for – integrating all three in glorious Technicolor swirl of Godly intervention.

Task 1: Words

Why *are* you a Christian? If someone were to ask you right now, could you explain yourself clearly? What's more, have you thought through your faith, have you begun to grapple with the difficult concepts and moved on from believing simply because it 'feels right'? Spend some time thinking about these things as well as browsing the shelves of a Christian bookshop. Try finding out more about who Jesus is, why he came to earth and what his death and resurrection means right now.

Task 2: Works

How does your faith get expressed through your actions? Are you a fighter for justice or are you just another consumer? Are you defending the rights of the oppressed or are you worried about what people might think? Get hold of a copy of *Upwardly Mobile* by David Westlake and read it, thinking of ways in which you might be able to make a difference through your lifestyle.

Task 3: Wonders

Does God have room to move through your life? Are you praying for opportunities for God to do the miracles while you're in the area? Try getting in the habit of praying as you go about your life, chatting to God and asking the Holy Spirit to provide you with opportunities to speak and to inspire you with the words to say. Remember: this bit's all about God; we're just the servants.

11

Go

(another chapter about evangelism)

Then the eleven disciples went to Galilee, to the mountain where Jesus had told them to go. When they saw him, they worshipped him; but some doubted. Then Jesus came to them and said, 'All authority in heaven and on earth has been given to me. Therefore go and make disciples of all nations, baptising them in the name of the Father and of the Son and of the Holy Spirit, and teaching them to obey everything I have commanded you. And surely I am with you always, to the very end of the age.'

(Matt. 28:16–20)

This is an account of the last words that Jesus spoke to the disciples before he returned to heaven. Today, the Great Commission is as powerful and relevant to us as it was to Jesus' audience two thousand years ago. In fact, we exist as Christians partly because of the extent to which the group of twelve took Jesus' command seriously. Like a line of dominoes, each generation inherits parts of the character and reaps the rewards of the previous generation's work. If we want to see the gospel interacting on a greater level with the rest of the world, the responsibility lies with us. If we squander the chance to follow Jesus' simple instruction, we not only risk opportunities today, but we erase them for tomorrow.

To live the life means to spend time in worship of the King, to allow time and space for the Holy Spirit to heal and empower us, but it is all meaningless if we stand with boots of lead, immovable and apathetic. When the passion witnessed in the meeting is fused with action outside, then our words have integrity and our deeds have power. We need to learn to give away what we've received.

Two breakthroughs

I recently spent a few months getting increasingly excited and frustrated about the whole 'Go' concept (excited because I wanted to do it, frustrated because I had built up my life without doing it). This particular time of change was marked by two separate events.

The first happened at Spring Harvest 1997. Matt Redman and I met up with the World Wide Message Tribe for a bit of chit-chat. Neither of us anticipated what would happen during those two hours. God ambushed us. As we all talked about what our hopes were for the future, each one of us felt that the Lord was doing something inside. We all realised again how much God has given us, and the only response is to get our hands dirty. When we understand that God doesn't give us gifts so that we can let them go old and stale, then we look at our gifts and talents in a totally different way. It is no longer possible to stay within our comfort zones. God is infinitely practical and makes his power available where the need is greatest. I left that meeting a changed man.

The second event couldn't have been more different. Instead of being surrounded by people, I was alone. Instead of God brewing up an intense and tangible atmosphere over an afternoon, I spent time quietly thinking about things and eating pizza. While staying at a friend's home in Dorset I read through the Acts of the Apostles. As I read, I asked God what the differences were between the first Church and ourselves. I was amazed at the answer: this must have been the fiftieth time I had read the book, and it was only now that I felt I really understood. The answer was this:

the difference between the first Church and ours lay not in their power-encounters with the Holy Spirit or in their theological education, but in their obedience to the command to go and tell others about him.

Obeying the command was their main priority, and they were sure to follow through when things were tough as well as when they were easy. When they were met with persecution, they went out to the lost with as much eagerness as when their message was met with thanks and joy. It all kicked off at Pentecost when they preached the gospel for the first time – assisted by the Holy Spirit. For a first attempt the boys didn't do too badly, notching up three thousand men as converts to Christianity. If it had been me I would have demanded a few warm-up gigs before I risked it in front of that many people, but the apostles knew that they were to do what Jesus had told them, so out they went.

Afterwards Peter and John were on their way to the temple when they met a beggar. Those of you who paid attention earlier will recognise their reply: 'Silver and gold I do not have, but what I have I give you. In the name of Jesus Christ of Nazareth, walk' (Acts 3:6). The beggar did what he was told and left walking and jumping, praising God for what he had done.

Not surprisingly, the Pharisees and teachers of the law were not happy about all this, and they had Peter and John arrested and beaten. The apostles were given an ultimatum: quit preaching the gospel or die. Peter and John returned to the others and got on with praying about the rather sticky situation. It is at this point that they blow a Christian like me out of the water. Instead of adopting a Pilavachi-esque technique like 'Oh Lord, please help us cos we're in trouble,' they turned to the Lord and asked for boldness to proclaim so that they might get right back out there and kick butt. As they prayed, the Holy Spirit came and filled them. God's presence was so real that even the walls shook.

Then there was a guy called Steven. He proclaimed Jesus so frequently and with such passion that the authorities had him stoned to death. He was the first Christian martyr and his death set off an increase in the hostilities against the early Christians. They were soon scattered all over the surrounding area, having fled from Jerusalem. On arrival in locations throughout Judea and Samaria, instead of lying low and trying not to get themselves killed, the apostles got stuck in once again, healing, teaching and spending time with people. They took his command seriously, and turned the world upside down.

As I read the book of the Acts of the Apostles I had to repent of something I have often said. I used to believe that the Acts of the Apostles should be called the Acts of the Holy Spirit, because it's all about the work of the Holy Spirit. I don't think that any more; it should be called the Acts of the Apostles because the apostles acted. They did something, they made a difference, and I believe God is telling us today to go and to make a difference in whatever way, big or small. The importance does not depend on the amount of people who witness our activity, but on the very fact that we obey our calling. It is about time that we took this seriously and were prepared to act like those disciples that we claim to admire.

Looking for a blessing

It was not too long ago that Christians were hopping on planes and heading for Toronto to receive whatever spiritual blessings were on offer. That has been followed by gatherings in Pensacola which encouraged thousands of people to recommit themselves to Christ. Both of these locations have seen the Lord move in power, yet I find it has a bittersweet taste. I love to see God move in power, and it makes me very excited to see the people of God hungry for more of him. Yet what I discovered while meeting with the Tribe, and then while I was on my own in Dorset, was that revival doesn't come when we go across the ocean to receive a blessing; it comes when we go across the street to *be* a blessing. The salvation of our nation lies, not surprisingly, in our hands. If we choose to value our neighbours by offering them a full range of practical expressions of the gospel, the chances are they will be a lot more inclined to hear what we have to say than if we show them our slides from the latest overseas location of blessing.

The Scriptures are full of exhortations for God's people to go, and at times I have been puzzled; bearing in mind that Jesus repeated himself so often on the subject, what part of the command do we have a problem with? Is it the G or the O? Like much of our faith, the basis is very simple, and is applicable to absolutely everybody.

Go with the flow

At times the outpouring of the Holy Spirit has been likened to the river mentioned in Ezekiel 47. It is a great picture of a river that flows out from the altar (the place of sacrifice, the cross). After a while the water is ankle-deep, then knee-deep, then up to the waist and then finally it is over the head. At that point it is impossible to walk; you need to swim. The river symbolises the Spirit of God, and it can be taken as an encouragement not just to paddle in God's Spirit, nor to wade, but to go all the way and give in to the power of God in our lives. The important question is, where is the river going? We need to allow God's Spirit to take us where he wants us to go, giving over control of our lives to him.

God wants to be the boss of his people; he wants more than our attendance at meetings, he wants our whole lives. Ezekiel 47 tells us that the river was going to the sea, to make the salt waters fresh. It was going out into the world, and where the river flowed there would be lots of fish and fruit trees growing along the shore. In the Bible, fish symbolise non-Christians, which is why Jesus told Peter and Andrew that he would make them fishers of men. If we also want to see life re-injected into the world, we need to follow the river and find the fish.

The choice to stay within the Church will inevitably lead to a misty-eyed retrospective of The Glory Days; like nostalgia for ration books and blackouts, we will look back on Toronto and recall how we shook, barked, roared and squealed. Whatever happened to those days, we will ask ourselves. The answer will be short and simple; the Spirit of God moved out into the world and we Christian Muppets have stayed in the Church.

How do we Go?

Jesus announced the beginning of his ministry (in Luke 4) with the words: 'The Spirit of the Lord is on me because he has anointed me to preach good news to the poor. He has sent me to proclaim freedom for the prisoners and recovery of sight for the blind, to release the oppressed; to proclaim the year of the Lord's favour.'

This was his manifesto. He came to preach the good news of forgiveness and salvation, to proclaim freedom and to bring healing and release from oppression. He came to bring social justice. This good news was for the poor, not simply the poor in spirit but the financially and materially poor. The freedom was for those unjustly imprisoned; the release was for those who were under the yoke of oppression; the year of the Lord's favour was the time when debts were cancelled and slaves set free.

Jesus did not simply proclaim this good news, he WAS the good news. He didn't stop at sympathising with the poor and oppressed, he became one of them. Jesus was God become poor. He spent time with the 'publicans and sinners' and treated them gently while he treated the Pharisees and teachers of the law harshly.

We must imitate Jesus' actions when he talked to the Samaritan woman at the well in John 4. She was an outcast and Jesus had plenty of time for her. So must we.

There is a chance that this strikes a chord with you but you are left feeling confused and unsure about the very nature of Going – just how, you may wonder, is it done? Fortunately there is no hierarchy here; we all have a chance to express God to others – it is not something that we leave to the evangelists. For every person for whom God is a stranger there is an endless combination of words, works and wonders that they will find relevant. The key to loving our neighbour (or those we have contact with), the starting block on which all else is built, is this: friendship. Without genuine friendship our words are distant, our works are hollow and the wonders don't have much to work through.

We can start with our families. Sometimes it seems it would be easier to go to Australia and evangelise than to stay back and live the life among those people who know us best, and who see us at our worst.

The poor are all around us. Whether their poverty is defined by finance, relationship, health or faith, there are many out there. In the same way we can give via our wallet, our time, our energy or skills. From a random act of kindness to a full-on regular commitment, God is ready to put our action to use.

A group of people on our training course noticed that the bus stop opposite their house regularly had elderly people waiting at it in the cold. They decided to take some chairs out for them to sit on and some coffee to drink. There was no ulterior motive – they didn't make the old biddies listen to a talk on the seven spiritual laws in return for the favour – they were simply doing what they (and we) have been told. After all, we Christians are supposed to be the nicest, most generous, most considerate people on the face of the earth.

Another bunch decided that one evening they would go down the road and wash people's cars. They didn't take any money and didn't draw parallels between the cleansing nature of the sponge and the water and the redeeming power of the cross and the Son. It was a nice thing to do, and they did it.

Part of belonging to a Western culture means that we also have a responsibility to look out for those who, by chance of birth, have inherited less than us. Organisations like Tear Fund, Toy Box or Amnesty International make it easy to get involved, producing detailed information on their projects. I once heard of a Christian who had refused to sign a petition to wipe out Third World debt because they did not feel that the Lord had called them to it. If their reason for refusing had been political I would have felt differently, but as it was the news left me sad. The truth is that we have been called. It is all there in black and white, the G and the O, the Great Commission, the call to set the captives free and be good news to the poor. There is no need to wait – some of us have been waiting for too long already. Our time on earth is not a practice run, it is the real thing, and the only chance we will ever get to be a light in the darkness. We do not have the luxury of saying 'no' to God.

My prayer is that we are immersed in the power, love and glory of Jesus and that it has the same effect on us that it had on the apostles. I pray that we might be missionaries in our homes, in our schools, in our places of work, in our community and in our nation. We need to care for our town, we need to care for our world, and that care needs to be expressed in very practical ways.

I heard a story of an American who decided to experiment with random acts of kindness. Whenever he arrived at a toll booth he would give twice the fee he owed and tell the attendant that he was paying for the car behind. The toll attendant assumed that he was travelling in a convoy and was paying for his friend, rather than a complete stranger. He loved watching in his rear-view mirror as the toll attendant tried to explain to a confused motorist why this guy had paid for him.

When a group of us were in South Africa I shared this as an example in a talk. The very next day we were driving around and we came to a toll booth. A wonderful friend suggested that I take a leaf out of my own book and pay for the guy behind. I tried to explain the difference between using an example in a talk and actually doing it, but the poor fool just couldn't grasp it. Eventually I gave in and gave the attendant twice the fee, telling him that it was also for the next car. As we drove away, I slowed down and looked in the rear-view mirror. We all got excited because our follower seemed to be a particularly suspicious one, and took quite some convincing that we were for real. As they left I went even slower so that we could all wave as they went past. They waved at us and mouthed, 'Thank you.' I felt like a true spiritual hero.

A few days later we had another go at it, but this time the person who was lucky enough to be behind us didn't even look at us as he passed. I wanted to chase him down and give him a slap. Then I realised the point, and remembered that it was to be like Jesus, not to give my ego a boost. Jesus often showed love to those who ignored him; if we are honest, we all spend a fair bit of time taking whatever he gives without saying thanks.

While reading this book you may have spotted a couple of references to Mother Teresa. I consider myself to be quite a fan of her life, yet like all good role-models, hearing about things she said and did often leaves me feeling uneasy; I flinch as her sacrificial life highlights my own selfishness. Somebody once asked why she bothered doing what she did, bearing in mind that all the people she helped could only ever be a drop in the ocean. Yes, she replied, but the ocean is made up of many drops. Nothing we do for Jesus in the world is insignificant; God's ocean is made up of many drops and, like the hairs on our heads, each one is seen and known. Whatever you do, God wants to empower you, to help you do it again and again.

Let's have another go at reading the story that Jesus told about judgment:

Then the King will say to those on his right, 'Come, you who are blessed by my Father; take your inheritance, the kingdom prepared for you since the creation of the world. For I was hungry and you gave me something to eat, I was thirsty and you gave me something to drink, I was a stranger and you invited me in, I needed clothes and you clothed me, I was sick and you looked after me, I was in prison and you came to visit me.'

Then the righteous will answer him, 'Lord, when did we see you hungry and feed you, or thirsty and give you something to drink? When did we see you a stranger and invite you in, or needing clothes and clothed you? When did we see you sick or in prison and go to visit you?'

The King will reply, 'I tell you the truth, whatever you did for one of these brothers of mine, you did for me.'

(Matt. 25:34–40)

We cannot divorce worship and justice; the Bible shows them glued together. The songs we sing must result in a change in the lives we live. For those who are unsure, it is worship to feed the hungry, it is worship to clothe the naked, it is worship to bless the homeless and to give them a home. All this is worship because Jesus said when we did it to one of the lowest, we did it to the highest. Can we see Jesus out in the world beyond the Church? Can we bless him, worship him with our lives, and not just with our words?

However, this is a challenge, and a hard one at that. Agreeing to Go does not guarantee a sugar-sweet passage through life, yet this is our time, our chance to do it right. We might be praying for revival – a good thing – but let's live it out, let's take the gospel of Jesus to our broken and hurting world.

Live it!

There's so much to say and yet so little as well. Just do it. Go on; do something, no matter how big or small, just do it. Pay for the guy behind you at the toll booth. Take a meal round to the old person living down your road. Get together with some friends and make sure you invite the person who is always on the fringes, the person that never fits in.

But then there's the other side, the one that we'd rather not admit. I'm sure I'm not alone in thinking that this all sounds like a lot of hassle – good hassle, but hassle nevertheless. I catch myself wishing that evangelism was merely a case of dragging someone along to a meeting, handing out a tract or giving a brief testimony before I leave the table. Wouldn't it all be so much easier if evangelism was something we could switch on, a suit we could climb into for a performance and then climb out of again at the end, going back to the anonymity of before?

Jesus wasn't like that. Instead of treating people as targets, he saw them as loved by God. Instead of talking to people out of duty, we see him responding to people with passion. Instead of giving a performance to a multitude, he lived his life with a handful of people close and personal, sharing his heart with them. And this is the point of the theory of 'go': we could look for a list of activities to work through but it would be a wrong turn. Instead we must recognise that the best we do is try to be authentic, committed, passionate, worshipping followers of Jesus, the kind who have followed his example and who find themselves living their lives in view of those who need to see him most.

Task 1

It's not just to Jesus that we have to look for top-notch examples: spend time looking at how people like Job, Gideon, Joseph, Abraham and David chose to live their lives. What was it about them that set them apart? What were the attitudes that they held towards God and others? Are there any aspects of their characters that you would like to aim for in your own life? Make a wish list of ways in which you'd like to grow in your relationship with God.

Task 2

Being able to 'go' starts with a realisation that it is on God that we are 100 per cent reliant. Get in the habit of meeting with God and leaving all your ambitions, hopes, fears and worries with him. Allow the Holy Spirit room to guide and prompt you as you go about your day.

12

How far should we go?

(being part of the culture)

Is Christianity going through an image crisis? Do we owe it to our children to take on the job of bringing Jesus into the next millennium with world-wide sponsorship deals, a funky new logo and his own brand of cola? Face it, two thousand years is a long time for anybody to keep the same wardrobe: I don't care what others may say, staffs, sandals and smocks have gone for good. Should the Church be like every other successful company, where the customer is king, to be enticed in whatever ways are necessary to get the sale?

Or perhaps you take another opinion: Christians never had it so good as when the pews were lined with burning coals, the services lasted eighteen hours and you could always be guaranteed a good witch-hunt at the end. Is it up to the Church to plough forward (regardless of what century the service was written in), providing onlookers with a fine example of tradition, history and a dignity long forgotten in these Nintendo days?

This isn't going to surprise anyone, but I make my camp somewhere in the middle of these two opinions. They are both a bit right and a lot stupid, which is probably a fairly good description of most of us when it comes to the issue of bringing God and our culture together.

So how culturally relevant should we be?

The question has caused more sulks and splits within the Church than many others. At the heart it can be divided

into two separate questions: should the Church change its style to make it more accessible? Should the Church change its message to fill up the pews?

Jesus did tell us how to pray, but thankfully he didn't mention anything about rainbow sweaters, pipe organs or songs about rowing boats – that doesn't mean we can't have them in church, just that suggesting trying things without them is not an offence punishable by death.

Jesus (the one on whose life we are basing our own) made sure that what he said was easily understood by his audience. That doesn't mean that he spoke v-e-r-y s-l-o-w-l-y, making sure he used his hands a lot, and always gave out printed notes afterwards. What Jesus did was to talk about situations and issues that everyone had come across already. For example, the language which Jesus spoke in was Aramaic. If you were after a really pure hit, you could get wound up by the fact that the first Christians dared to translate Jesus' words into Greek. Their reason for changing the language was that Aramaic was slipping down the charts, being replaced by Greek as the In Language. Today there is only one village on top of a hill somewhere in Syria that still speaks Aramaic. If they hadn't changed the language the gospel would only be understood in that village. The first disciples changed the packaging to fit the people.

Paul said, 'I have become all things to all men so that by all possible means I might save some' (1 Cor. 9:22b). This doesn't mean that he saw the gospel of Christ as a giant pic'n'mix, where each punter could have whatever suited their pleasure best. Paul was all things to all people in the way he communicated. Like Jesus, he made sure that he was understood. Jesus communicated in a way that was culturally relevant to his day; his story-telling was not for the benefit of an audience that was a bit slow, but because everybody used stories and parables as part of their normal conversations. When he said, 'I am the bread of life,' it was because bread was the staple diet. When, at the last supper, he took the bread and the wine and blessed it, saying, 'This is my body . . . this is my blood,' he was holding their equivalent of a Big Mac and a Diet Coke.

Sheep and fish

Jesus taught about sheep because he talked to lots of people who spent time around sheep. He spoke about fish because there were lots of people listening to him who made their living from the sea. The subjects he picked were vital parts of his culture. Jesus also talked about taxes, landowners and wedding banquets, but when he spoke about these he was in Jerusalem – where the fishermen, shepherds and farmers would have been replaced with those who made their living in other ways. The parable of the net in Matthew 13 put across a similar message in the country as the parable of the wedding banquet (Matthew 22) did in the city. Jesus is the King of kings, Lord of lords and Captain of communication. He picked his words carefully to have maximum impact, showing each person that his message was for them. Two thousand years later and society has changed beyond all recognition: the industrial and technological revolutions have brought us to a new place, with new needs, new hurts and new horizons. What do we Christians talk about? Sheep and fish.

It is important to understand the language of Scripture, to find out what it meant then and what it means now, and there is something enlightening about exploring the culture in which Jesus lived, but we mustn't confuse our study with our outreach. Part of talking about issues that relate to people's lives means that we hopefully become a genuine part of that culture, just like Jesus did when he was in rural as well as urban areas.

Get off my land

The danger for the Church has often been that we form our own church culture. It can become as much of a clique as a golf club, a local political party or the cool group in the playground. These days I think God is challenging his people to actually care for the world so much that we make ourselves accessible to it. The gospel – with its no-compromise message of morality, purity and forgiveness – is on its own an offence to the 'Me' culture of today; God doesn't need us to be snotty and offensive on top of it. We owe it, to God and to all his children, to ask ourselves whether the way we do things leaves people confused and uninterested or interested and welcome. When people come to our churches, are they met with strange rituals and mumbled jargon or do they find us easy to understand? This may start you off thinking about traditional churches, but things are just as bad, if not worse, in some of our modern charismatic churches. We have all manner of styles and practices that can seem so bizarre to the outsider. If we are serious about following Jesus, we will be sure to follow his lead and be ready to take the message out to as many different people as possible.

I was recently talking to a fashion photographer and I asked her why, as a Christian, she was involved in an industry that seemingly contradicts so much of the gospel. She told me that it was what she felt called to. She told me that through her work she had been able to treat people with more dignity and respect than they were used to. She knew that she had been called to do her job well, and found that Jesus was as relevant to the fashion culture as he was to those who sleep on the streets.

A guy in our church had an idea to set up a club in the middle of town, playing the sort of music that he loves (and the sort that I think is just too fast to do anything to). His reason was that it was his culture and he loved it.

A little while back we set up an after-school club in our warehouse. For three afternoons a week about thirty children, whose parents can't afford to pay for childcare, come along and have time and energy devoted to them. The reason for this is simple: Jesus told us to get involved with our culture.

This is the beautiful thing about Christianity: high fashion, hyperactive eight-year-olds and drum and bass may not have a whole load in common with each other, but God is so wide, so creative, that he makes each one of us with different passions. The gospel is so powerful and good that it relates to everyone, it's not bound by culture. These are the best places from which to evangelise; follow an instinct or whatever excites, and we meet like-minded people and can make friendships and talk about the gospel in ways that are relevant.

To the beat of a different drum

On the other hand, there are certain things that we are meant to be counter-cultural about. When the early Christians translated Jesus' words from Aramaic they changed the packaging, but they made sure they left the gift intact. While Jesus changed the stories, he never deviated from the message he came to give. That message is a challenge to many aspects of culture; instead of selfishness it talks about generosity; instead of sexual freedom it talks about purity; instead of death being a kind of nothingness it talks about heaven and hell. Sometimes we are meant to be prophetic to the culture, not to be so absorbed in it that we are indistinguishable from it. On certain issues we are supposed to speak out and say if something is wrong. The way we do this, though, is not by pointing the finger and condemning, but by living a different life and showing that we care by getting stuck in.

Where, in our culture, there is greed, we need to live lives of incredible generosity. Where there is a high abortion rate, we need to be there to help single mothers. Where there is crime and vandalism, we need to train and equip people to support themselves with dignity. The Sermon on the Mount is the last word in living against the culture; love your enemies, do good to those who hate you (Luke 6:27), give and it will be given to you, pressed down, shaken together, running over, it will be poured into your lap (Luke 6:38). As Jesus said it then, it's still relevant to today – it still goes against the grain. That's what makes real Christianity attractive, because it's something unique, it's something beautiful and pure.

We've gone wrong in the past by presenting the gospel in a way that's totally alien to society, but have matched the rest of society for greed, ambition and selfishness. Perhaps we have avoided saying the F-word, or have managed to wrap ourselves up in tradition and religion and call it Being A Good Christian. The fact remains that we have missed the point.

We have to think long and hard about the areas in which we need to be relevant to people – we can't please all of them all the time – and we also need to put plenty of energy into working out what they need to know about Jesus. But some things don't change; Jesus did die on a cross, he did rise again, he did die for our sins. These truths can't change, they are the Christian message, but how we communicate that message needs to change for different cultures.

Live it!

To talk to certain more mature members of our society today you'd think that today's generation of teenagers were the first ones ever in the history of the world to want to change anything. But of course it's all part of the natural process: people want to change things in their youth, reacting against the failings of the previous generation. Just when they've got used to having things the way they like them, along come another generation who want to go and mess it all up again. Typical.

I reckon it's useful to keep this in mind when thinking about culture; let's not fall into the trap of thinking that it's our job to make Christianity cool, or that the ways we find of expressing our worship are any more valid than those used in the past. No, the aim of the game is to remain faithful to the commandment Jesus gave his followers: to go and make disciples of all nations. We're not here to make spectators of all nations, to make impressed punters or overawed onlookers; we're here to make disciples, and that means establishing and developing relationships.

Ah yes, relationships. Funny things, relationships. Why? Because you can't fake them. People have a knack of smelling a phoney a mile off. And this means that we must value those that fall across our paths. It means that we must value the culture of which we are a part, relating to people in a way that is authentic and genuine, understanding the struggles within it and communicating the essential and immovable truths about the life of Jesus.

So there we have it: holding two opposites in balance. We don't need to be ashamed of our faith yet we should not deny the part our culture has played in shaping us. We don't need to twist our faith so that it becomes just another fashion accessory and we don't need to deny the differences that exist between the rules of the world and the message of the cross.

Task 1

We need to learn to take a step back from our culture and recognise what are the healthy and unhealthy influences it exerts on us. To help you do this, take a selection of magazines, songs, programmes and films that are popular in the sub-section of culture you move in. Think about them long and hard (if possible, read, listen to and watch them again). Try and watch them with a stranger's eyes and try to find answers to these questions: what are the messages you get from them about sex and relationships? What are the messages you get about money and ambition? What sort of attitudes do they hold about poverty, injustice and greed? How does friendship get portrayed and expressed?

Task 2

We also need to remember that Christianity has plenty to say about the world we live in. With a friend try looking through a newspaper and discussing how you might react as a Christian to the events that are going on in the world around you. It will be easy enough if you come across stories about wars, famine or debt, but does your faith give you anything to say on issues like the environment, medicine, education or technology? You and your friend might like to talk these through with someone older whose opinions you respect.

13

Where should we go?

(what is your calling in life?)

I always used to think of myself as being like one of the kids from Fame. Perhaps it was before your time (if it was be sure to ask someone who does remember), but each episode started with Miss Lydia Grant sitting backwards on an old chair, wearing excessively large leg-warmers and banging her stick on the ground as she emphasised the creed that she imparted to all those deeply soulful pupils: 'You want fame? Well, fame costs, and here's where you start paying – in sweat.' I always felt a rush of excitement as those who were younger and less well-endowed in the leg-warmer department opened their eyes wide and prepared to work like Trojans, for the next thirty minutes, towards the ultimate goal: fame.

My reasons for comparing myself with 'the kids' may not be immediately obvious, but the truth must be known; my rush of emotion at the beginning of the show was not in anticipation of my landing the lead role in a Broadway show, it was at the small thought that I too might one day do something great, and do it for God. While Leeroy, Denise and Bruno had visions of landing themselves a big job with a fat pay cheque, I was coming up with rough concepts for my 'Mike Pilavachi, Man Of Faith' World Tour.

In those days I was generally a bit rough around the edges of my faith. While I meant well enough, when my enthusiasm met my inexperience the consequences were often amusing. I thought that my goal was the Christian spotlight, and if I wanted it with as much single-minded passion as the Famesters I would surely end up satisfied.

I later found out that I was wrong. I found this verse: 'Whatever you do, work at it with all your heart, as working for the Lord, not for men, since you know that

you will receive an inheritance from the Lord as a reward'
(Col. 3:23–4)

It says it all to me. Many of us think that to work full-
time for Christ means working full-time for the Church. I
had wanted the glitz and the glamour of church work – a
bit of me had wanted people to look at me and think, 'There
goes Mike, he gets paid to be holy' – but my heart was
(kind of) in the right place. I genuinely thought that being
a missionary was the only way to use your work life in a
God-pleasing way. I had to wait from when I was sixteen
until I was twenty-nine before I went into what I thought
was full-time Christian work. Looking back, I'm convinced
that I wasted those years. I was too busy waiting for the
calling to come from Africa to realise that God was trying
to use me in Harrow. Calling, I have since found out, is all
about the present, and consequently wherever you are there
is a call of God to do his will.

What is full-time Christian work?

My confusion started with a simple misunderstanding of
the facts. What I thought was full-time Christian work can
be described as full-time church work, because every Christian who is living as a disciple of Jesus is into full-time
Christian work; when we belong to him, everything we do
belongs to him – not only our money, but our time. Whatever we do, we should see it as our calling, otherwise there
is little point in us being there. Church is full of people who
feel stuck in a job they feel they have no calling to, waiting
for the right job to come along. There really is no time like
the present for knuckling down and doing things that
please God's heart.

I feel slightly ashamed of myself when I think of how I
wasted the first seven years of my secular employment. I
started on a temporary contract and remained on one despite the fact that I was offered numerous chances to sign

up to something a bit more permanent. My attitude to the job spread over in my attitude to the staff; after all, I thought, I'll be in Africa before long, so it would be silly to develop any really deep friendships. It was only in the last two years there that I saw sense and realised what a fool I'd been. I decided that my career was worthy of God; and so started to put more effort in. Soon after, I began to get promotions and got to know my colleagues on a deeper level than before. Then God stepped in.

Divine punishment or humour, I'm not sure which, but this was the time that God decided to finally offer me a chance to get involved in some full-time church work. What I had spent almost twelve years dreaming of, placing on a pedestal and considering to be sheer perfection was now a sacrifice. Giving up the job meant much more than escaping from the boredom of secular work. I did quit my job, but I know that those final two years helped me to mature. I'm also sure that, had I decided to stay there, God would have used me and called me to express his nature in the middle of the office.

Widening the view

Sometimes, being at school, at college or in secular work is tough. It can be hard when we are confronted by a range of issues that seem totally alien to the Sunday service. While a job as seemingly mundane as putting out the chairs before the church meeting can easily be thought of as useful, the work of an accountant is slightly harder to spiritualise. The secular worker is faced with all manner of internal questions about their job: is it valid? is it making a difference? how does it count in the grand scheme of things?

The problem here stems from a twisted view of what God wants. The reason for writing a chapter like this is to challenge the myth that if your employer doesn't incorporate a little fish in their logo then your job can't be serving the Lord. Our value system has ignored relationship and the preaching of the gospel 'if necessary using words' (remember St Francis of Assisi?) and replaced it with a strange notion that the Church is not only a hospital, training ground and a home, but an employment agency too. Think for a minute about the model that Jesus gave us; it was all about relationship, all about living the life.

Accountancy may not call upon the skills of biblical insight that may be required of a man or woman of the cloth. However, line up the spiritual gifts and it's plain to see that they can be incorporated into any workplace.

Prophecy doesn't have to come packaged with the words, 'I feel the Lord is saying to you . . .' or 'I was just watching you at the photocopier and God told me . . .' Cut the religious jargon, and what are you left with? Talking to people and using a little common sense about injecting those spiritual hunches into the conversation.

Pastoring goes beyond 'So just how *is* your walk with the Lord, Gerald?' On a basic level it is caring for people and encouraging their development – a fine description of a good colleague.

Evangelism can take many forms, but statistically most people get to know Jesus through friendship with a Christian. If you've managed to work on the first two gifts then you will have established a caring, attentive relationship, out of which either your colleague will want to know about your faith or you can let them know bit by bit.

Our faith, the thing that we are living for, is more than capable of being relevant in any situation you care to mention. We have no need to be afraid of taking on jobs in areas the Church has traditionally shied away from. As Christians, do we believe in walking on the other side and letting Satan do whatever he wants? Today we need to get in there as Christians, to be salt and light actually in the world just as much as we needed to when Jesus first commanded us two thousand years ago. Yes, God does call a few to serve and equip those who are out working in the world, but they are the exception, not the rule. The rest of us have our default setting out there working in the non-churched world. It's there that we can get on with the business of imitating Christ, making friendships with those we meet.

If there's nothing else we do when we are in secular employment, we should be making friendships, treating people with dignity and respect. We should be asking God to help out when things are tough instead of running away. The presence of opposition and difficulty is a sure sign that something is going right. Whether we choose to be a shop assistant, a fashion photographer, a teacher or a lawyer, God has a way of using his people for his glory. After all, as servants of the King we only have a limited amount of borrowed time with which to shine our light in the darkness.

The spice of life

Becoming a Christian doesn't mean having a lobotomy, and there are all manner of situations that we need to use our brains in when we sign up for secular employment. We will encounter situations where our values come up against opposition, which puts us in roughly the same position as the early Church – and look what they achieved. This is where the unity and community of Christianity come into play. The job of those who are in full-time church work is described in Ephesians 4 verse 11:

> It was he who gave some to be apostles, some to be prophets, some to be evangelists, and some to be pastors and teachers, to prepare God's people for works of service so that the body of Christ may be

built up until we all reach unity in the faith and in the knowledge of the Son of God and become mature, attaining to the whole measure of the fulness of Christ.

The reason for handing out all these jobs (leaders, prophets, evangelists, pastors, teachers) is simple: so that the body of Christ might be built up, that God's people (the saints) might be equipped to serve out there in the world. Following on from that, we can see that the job of an evangelist is not simply to do all the evangelism, but to train the Church to do the evangelism where they are. The job of a pastor is not simply to pastor everybody in the Church but to raise up people with pastoral gifts so that they can better encourage others. Those positions in the Church are simply for people who have those gifts in abundance, and who are there to equip the Church to do the work. The apostles, prophets, pastors, teachers and evangelists are not the ones who are meant to do the work – that job is for *all* the saints, the people of God.

When we talk about the ministry of this preacher or that worship leader, we should really be evaluating it by looking at the impact it has on those who hear it. The ministry is meant to happen out in the world, not in the Church.

Whose job is it anyway?

We have somehow got confused about what 'the ministry' of a church is. I can remember a well-known evangelist visiting our church many years ago. He was there to 'do' our evangelism for a while; all we had to do was bring a couple of unsaveds along and let him do the rest. I thought this was great; I could get all my evangelism for the year done in one meeting. It hadn't crossed my mind that I could use him as a tool to equip me to get out there – that would have seemed too much like hard work. Likewise the pastor's job is not to pastor everyone, the pastor's job is to make sure that everyone is pastored. Thankfully God seems to be raising up a generation who view church very much as a home and a resource, but one to go out from into the world.

I am excited by the prospect of seeing Christians doing the very best they can out in the world. The possibilities for a band getting into the charts, for example, getting out beyond the walls of the church, are endless. The opportunities for a nursing sister to affect the lives of the patients and nurses that he or she works with could also be huge, and equally pleasing to God. The principles are the same whether we are a musician, salesman, nurse or cleaner: do the best we can, celebrate the gifts that God has given us, live lives that are pleasing to God.

Paranoid or pious?

The media, for example, has traditionally been the object of much criticism by the Church. An industry that is built on the foundations of greed, image and sex has scared many of us off. Yet those are precisely the reasons why we should be involved, engaging with the culture and influencing the way the rest of the population is moulded and taught. If the media has treated us Christians harshly in the past, it could be because we have lacked the bottle to get stuck in. As a television director I met once said, Christians don't need to be so paranoid; there are plenty of open-minded people out there. Those that we consider to be out to persecute us are in the minority.

One of the hopes for revival in these days is that people will start to hear the call and go out and make a difference. The important question in such times is, 'How do I work out what my calling is?' Many of us get paranoid and worry about missing it or going down the wrong route, as if any error would lead us straight to hell. We remain paralysed with indecision and end up going nowhere. God is not like that. In one sense he gives us a choice. He hasn't made one narrow, poorly lit path for our lives, so that if we should trip up and miss out on being an actor or working in Boots or whatever then we lose the game. Sometimes he gives us choices and says, 'Go for it – what's on your heart?'

Obviously we must be slightly careful on this one; no matter how right it feels, I would view a desire to follow a career as a lap-dancer as a bit suspicious. I recently heard someone describe the way to know what your calling is: when a long-felt desire meets an opportunity. If that happens to you and you spend time praying about it, don't waste time waiting for the heavens to send you your own personal confirmation written in the clouds, have a go and trust God to shut the doors if it doesn't work out.

This may be all very well if you have a desire to do something or a hunch about where your gifts lie, but for many of us the minute we try and think about the future our minds blank out. Ironically this is an excellent place in which to be. Think of it as a blank canvas rather than a dead end; pray for God to inspire and install a passion in the heart. If we do believe that God is God, the ultimate creator of all life, then we must believe that everything (and everybody) has a purpose. Even if the situation you find yourself in is bland and uninspiring, it is worth avoiding the temptation to give up on God's calling. As we see with David, the seemingly unimpressive can be the most valuable training ground.

Manic Street Preachers

Perhaps by valuing our gifts without covering them with religion – learning how to preach the gospel in the same style as our Saviour, who lived a life full of actions, relevant parallels and (in the best possible way) goodness – we will discover a new relationship with the rest of the world. If we want to have a voice in the world, if we weep over the decline of standards, we should be involved in it. Shouting from the sidelines was never something that Jesus did. Instead, we should imitate his willingness to establish a relationship with the world. If we do want to be one of the shapers of our culture, we can't expect God to magically transport us in, regardless of our training or experience. We need to start at the bottom, like everybody else, with the media studies course, the membership of a political party, the contribution to a local paper or hospital radio. Alongside that, we need to encourage others to follow these paths and support them as they explore their calling.

The uncomfortable pedestal

When we see a Christian in the spotlight of the media or politics, we've often put them up on a pedestal and then accused them of selling out and missing opportunities to preach the gospel. Strangely we don't seem to get so excited about accountants or salespeople, accusing the perfume counter assistant of losing a potential convert as they leave the store with their purchases. Our lives are meant to witness and, where necessary, we are meant to be ready to give our reasons for living the life, but not to ram things down people's throats. Some he calls to out-and-out evangelism – we see that in the Scriptures; that's what Paul was, an evangelist as well as an apostle and a church-planter – but we're all meant to serve the Lord wherever he puts us. I think it's fantastic that nobody is quite certain just how much of a Christian Tony Blair is. He clearly has Christian principles and they influence his work, which suits me fine. I don't need him to do my evangelism for me, I don't need him to be a model at whom I can point and say, 'Well, Tony's one, so why shouldn't you be one, too?'

God is a big enough reason on his own to follow him. He doesn't need us down here as his PR people, tackling his oh-so-tricky image problem. What he does need is for us to obey him and fulfil the potential that he has placed within us. He needs us to worship, to listen, to act and to serve. The norm is to work in the secular world, the exception is the call to serve the rest of the Church from within. God loves what he has created so much that when we profess our love and desire to serve him he has a seemingly limitless set of opportunities for us to explore. What God wants is for us to live the life.

Live it!

I don't know why, but it seems that one of the hardest issues around is reinforcing the message about full-time Christian work not necessarily being full-time church work. And hey, I'm doing it myself, working for the church and all that. But no matter how much we say from the front that church is about the church staff supporting the rest of the congregation as they do the stuff out there in the world, the message has a hard time getting through. Some people still feel as if their job in Boots is less important to God than the post of Youth Worker, or that they would be so much more able to work 'for the Lord' if only they could ditch college and become a full-time worship leader. But take a look at Jesus and this kind of logic really fails to add up: there was a man who devoted himself to people who were often uninfluential and who rarely seemed to appreciate his true purpose. Yeah, there are stories of mass meetings where thousands were in attendance, but he poured most of himself into the relationships with the twelve men closest to him. He didn't die a celebrity's death.

Task 1

Matthew 25:31–46 is the sort of passage that could change your life. Actually, it's the sort of passage that *should* change your life. Read it to yourself out loud, taking time to look up any references that your Bible gives you to go with it. What are the criteria that are used to separate the sheep from the goats? Just what is Jesus saying to the disciples through it about how they should live their lives? Do you think that the same message given to them applies to you today?

Task 2

If feeding the poor, supporting the lonely, helping the sick and freeing the oppressed are the signs of knowing God, what sort of different ways could you imagine being able to serve God?

Task 3

I heard someone once suggest that you can work out your calling by matching your talents with the opportunities to use them in a way that pleases God. Take time to think through your talents. Then think through the options that are open to you to use those talents. Can you see ways of serving God down those paths? If you don't feel that there are any options open to you, pray and ask God to be at work in your life, opening up opportunities to you. Then it's up to you to get on, live the life and try out your calling.

14

Does God take Visa?

(a chapter about generosity)

I'm not sure why, but it's easy to feel funny when the subject of money comes up. As a Christian I get twitchy, nervous even, at the thought of it, as if by bringing it out into the open I admit that I have a problem with it. Like much of our faith, the teaching on it is perfectly clear and simple, but my reaction is pure confusion. The main question – am I generous enough? – can only ever call up one answer (and it's not yes), but after my sheepish reply come a thousand more questions: how much is enough? can I give too much? is it wrong to receive gifts and nice things? shouldn't I give it all away and live on the street? what do I really need to live on?

A group of us were in South Africa recently, travelling around different churches, taking meetings and all that sort of thing. We saw a lot of wealth, incredible countryside and a lot of poverty. You can probably tell what's coming next, but there was a church that we visited that made me completely change my view on giving. As we stood in the poorest church of the trip – a shack in the middle of thousands of other shacks, making up a township called Inanda – we saw people who had less to live on than we spend each year on cinema tickets giving away all they had. As the pastor announced the start of the collection I got into my UK Collection Mode: face as miserable as a bald hippie, hands as shy as a monk in a girls' dormitory. I looked around and saw that I was alone in my grumpiness; the church was full of the poorest people I had ever met, giving their money as they danced, sang and cried with joy. They knew, more than I had ever understood, exactly how much God had given them.

No set answers

There are no set answers to the questions about giving. There isn't an amount to give that puts us safely in the *Generous* category. What we can learn, though, is the attitude. There is a way of life that we see in the Bible that is a perfect model for us to follow.

Acts chapter 2 is one of those passages that we often read in church. At least once a year we dust it off and read all about what happened on the day of Pentecost, what many people call the birthday of the Church. On that day, 120 believers were gathered in an upper room in Jerusalem. They were praying hard because Jesus had told them to wait until the Holy Spirit came on them, giving them power to be witnesses in Jerusalem, Judea, Samaria and to the ends of the earth. Finally the day came for the Holy Spirit to turn up, and he descended like a dove, bringing with him what seemed like tongues of fire. Straight away they were filled with the Spirit, and they began to speak in other languages. They went into the streets, met by large crowds – who thought they were drunk, they seemed so happy – who were even more confused that these uneducated men could suddenly speak a variety of languages. Peter preached the gospel, and at the end told them that he and the other 119 weren't drunk, as they thought, but full of the Spirit of God. Three thousand men became Christians on the spot.

The story doesn't stop there. Being a bit of a showman, I was kind of disappointed when I first read the passage. How, I scoffed, did they ever think they could top that? Everybody knows, you save your best gags till last. As I read on I stopped criticising. The best bit follows, as it describes life after that day:

They devoted themselves to the apostles' teaching and
to the fellowship, to the breaking of bread and to
prayer. Everyone was filled with awe, and many wonders and miraculous signs were done by the apostles.
All the believers were together and had everything in
common. Selling their possessions and goods, they
gave to anybody as he had need. Every day they
continued to meet together in the temple courts. They
broke bread in their homes and ate together with glad
and sincere hearts, praising God and enjoying the
favour of all the people. And the Lord added to their
number daily those who were being saved.

(Acts 2:42–7)

What we could call the fruit of the Holy Spirit's visit to
them, the way that it changed their lives, was that God's
people devoted themselves. They became a group who
were committed to teaching and to fellowship, to breaking
bread and to praying. They had everything in common –
that doesn't mean that they all immediately liked the same
kind of music or food – they sold their possessions and
gave the proceeds away.

The first fruit of Pentecost was that the gospel was
preached powerfully. There was a display of God's supernatural power that blew people's minds and opened their
eyes. But what we are left with is not a Class of AD 30, a
group of Spirit Junkies talking through the glory days of
the ultimate rush. What they were left with was a desire to
be more generous, to be more like God.

The Scriptures are full of encouragements for us to be
more like God in our generosity. He keeps on giving, never
stopping for a breather, to stock up on blessings or to check
out what's happening on the other channels. God is love
and the nature of love is to give itself away. Look at the
Bible and it isn't hard to see plenty of examples of God

giving to his people: protection, freedom, children, healing. The biggest example has to be Jesus, the most precious, valuable thing that God had. The act of sending down his most precious child is the blueprint for us, a perfect model of how to live our lives. Jesus knew this, and in the Sermon on the Mount he told the disciples to give 'and it will be given to you ... pressed down, shaken together and running over, it will be poured into your lap'. Jesus also encouraged the disciples to be the kind of people who would give their time, money and possessions as part of their worship.

In his second letter to the Corinthians Paul says that God loves a cheerful giver (9:7). The Greek word for 'cheerful' literally means 'hilarious'; God doesn't just want us to give, he wants us to give with joy and with hilarity. God took great delight when Joash put a chest outside the temple courts (2 Chron. 24:10). All of the officials and people brought their contributions gladly, dropping them into the chest until it was full. The key word here is 'gladly' (or 'cheerfully'). In our society we are meant to be a prophetic people – that isn't a flowery way of saying that we need to shout at people as they wait their turn at the supermarket check-out, nor does it mean that we are to have all the personal hygiene awareness of a confused skunk – it means that we are supposed to show something different by our actions. The churchgoers of Inanda showed me something by their actions. As they gave cheerfully, their actions told me that, when it comes to possessions, attitude is everything. In a society that is so hung up on what it can get; what it would do with a Lottery jackpot, how much can be saved (or spent) each year, whether investments move up or down by a fraction of a per cent, we, God's people, must learn to live a different way, having a different attitude towards ownership. Holding tightly on to possessions is not God's way. When we see poverty we should give, when we see loneliness we should be offering hospitality. These things are a sign that God is alive, among us and interested in the world.

Tight fists or holy hands?

There have been talks given in church about stewardship, looking after God's money and resources. Sometimes I understand what they mean; it's about being wise about what we spend money on, making sure that it isn't blown on a night out in Vegas for all the pastoral staff. At other times, though, stewardship is just another word for being tight. God has plenty of cash and is the ultimate in generosity: can you, after all, seriously imagine anybody being more generous than God? He doesn't want us to be mean with our possessions, looking after them so carefully in case someone steals them; he wants us to give lots of what we have away.

What it's all about

A couple of years ago at the Soul Survivor conference, Steve Chalke spoke at one of the main evening meetings. He tackled the subject of justice, challenging people to be offended by poverty and motivated to do something about it. At the end, each person was invited to go back to their tent and find an item of clothing that they wanted to give away to homeless people in London. Together, people lined up in silence to give away what they had chosen. After thirty minutes there was a lorry full of clothes heading back to London.

I thought long and hard about that night. There was something in the atmosphere that made the occasion special. On the face of it, it was little different to putting coins in a collection box, but there was such a hush as the people lined up that that meeting became different. I soon realised what had happened: people weren't giving to the homeless (they knew hardly anything about them and Steve had only mentioned them right at the end of his talk), they were giving to God. It was one of the most intimate worship times I have ever experienced.

Yes, it is a good thing to be giving money away to the Church, to the poor, to charities, but as the story shows, the object of our giving really isn't those groups, it is God. When we give, we do it because God wants us to, because it pleases him. He gave us, free of charge, the life of his Son; that is what we respond to when our hand goes in our pocket, whoever ends up getting the cash. We are being like God, responding to his grace.

Mine vs God's

The secret of giving generously is to realise that it all belongs to God in the first place. When we become Christians a transaction takes place: we give our lives to God and he pays for them on the cross. When he bought us, it wasn't like a home-assembly wardrobe with half the bits missing. He got the whole kit, every part of our lives. He bought our finances, our clothes, homes, abilities and dreams. Every bit of us belongs to God.

It's great when we see things this way; it makes it so much easier for God to shift his possessions around. Three years ago a couple who I had never met came up to me and said that God had told them to give me their car. I was amazed; my car had broken down that week and I was about to arrange a suitable funeral for it. I was convinced they were on a wind-up, but they promised me they weren't. Then I realised what was going on; they were obviously about to give me their MOT failure, easing their consciences as they eased into the soft leather of a new BMW. But I thought it would be worth my while to have a look, and there was nothing to say that I couldn't sell it for scrap and walk away with £50 in my pocket.

They took me around the corner and pointed to what I can only describe as a Successful Man's Car. This was the sort of thing you drove if you had an Armani suit hanging up in the back, a car that said, 'Yes, I do have lots of credit cards, a six-foot-wide fridge and a stomach the size of East Anglia.' I liked it.

'The Lord bless you,' I said, trying my best not to go up and kiss it. I couldn't believe that they were giving it to me, but they said God had told them, and as far as they were concerned that was all that needed to be said.

I thanked them over and over, wondering whether they might expect me to do something in return, like keep it clean.

'The way I see it,' said the man, 'is that it's just like a chess board; God owns all the pieces and he's just moving them around.'

This was an amazing experience. Not only did I end up with a car that suited my waist size, I received a clear sign through his people that God loves and cares for me.

Right now you might be feeling a bit confused. How can I be banging on about giving it all away in one breath and drooling over a Vauxhall Carlton CD 2000 (ABS braking, CD player, power-assisted steering) the next? I'm not sure either, but I do know that God loves to give gifts. Before Jesus was even out of nappies he was given a range of exclusive and expensive gifts. Even living your whole life for Jesus doesn't repay the price he paid for all of us on the cross.

Perhaps the answer lies within us. We are all different, all in different situations with different levels of wealth. Apart from two people in this world, we all have someone who is better off, and someone who is worse off than us. What we can all do, though, is give. I'm into the discipline of tithing, giving away 10 per cent of whatever we have, but I think it wrong that once we've given God his tenth we think we can get on with the business of enjoying our 90 per cent. Instead, I think it better to ask God how much of his money we can keep. We belong to him, and everything that we have, everything that we are, belongs to him too. Done this way, being generous can really hurt. When we get to the stage when giving is painful, then we know we're headed in the right direction. While we may never get there, never be able to sit back and say, 'Yes, I give enough,' we will at least be facing the right way.

Yes, but does God take Visa?

Today, things like telephone banking, the Internet and credit cards make looking after and getting rid of cash something that can happen in an instant. Giving to God can seem a bit less convenient, a bit more of a hassle. Remembering to take the notes along to church is sometimes as hard as remembering to take the Bible. There are a million boulders that block our path, countless excuses to turn around and head home, giving up on the discipline of being generous, going soft on splashing out for God. 'Come into my life, Lord,' we say, and we show him around the place for the first time. We give him the full tour – memories, loves, pains and hopes – but quickly walk past the box in the corner where we stash the cash.

We won't think twice about splashing out on a McD's value meal gone large, but putting the equivalent cash in the collection basket can give us worse indigestion than a truck-load of manky fishburgers. Listlessly handing over the money on a Sunday seems so dull, so low on fun, that there can be little wonder we struggle with it.

Jesus said in Matthew 10 verse 38 that if anyone was up for following him, they had to take up their cross. That means putting down whatever else we're playing with and committing ourselves to going his way. Daily. This is what stops Christianity from being a fluffy, cuddly, sweet and lovely fortnight break when we've got a little tired, and takes it on to the next level. This is what stopped the post-Pentecost Church from being a bunch of lazy morons, turning them into a group that changed the world. When God has it all from us, Christianity becomes something that is real and effective. We need to give more than just our money: we need to learn to live generously with everything we have – time, energy, wisdom and love.

The Bible is stacked with teaching on wealth and poverty; it is the second most common topic in the Old Testament after idolatry. In the New Testament there are over five hundred verses of direct teaching on the subject; that's an incredible one in sixteen verses. Jesus talked more about wealth and poverty than he did about heaven and hell, sexual morality, the law or the Second Coming. One in every five verses in James' letter is about the relationship between the rich and the poor. In Luke's gospel it is one in every seven. In Mary's song (Luke 1:46–55) she says that with the coming of Jesus the mighty will be brought low, the rich sent away empty, the poor exalted and the hungry satisfied. Why talk about money so much? Because the Bible does.

The first Christians were people of mercy, giving to all who were in need. The believers in Jesus were known as 'the people of the way' before they were known as Christians. This was because of 'the way' that they lived. They weren't called the people of the belief, the people of the experience or the people of the party, but the people of the way. People will see the difference in us when we learn to be generous, to give when it hurts. It's part of our worship, it's part of our witness.

We started this chapter with me moaning about generosity being such a difficult issue to understand. I hope we've finished in a better place. There are no set answers, that much is true, but there is a rule: if it isn't hurting, it's not giving. At the end of the day, we've all been given so much that there are a thousand ways that we can give back to God. At some point it gets down to the subject of money, but before that it's all about attitude – to God, to others and to those consumer goods that make life just that little bit more comfortable.

Having a lifestyle of giving breaks the hold of materialism over us. (Materialism is to love and put your security in money and possessions.) Jesus tells us (Matt. 6:19–20) to make sure that we store treasures in heaven and not on earth. That means we are to live on earth with heaven in mind, and not our bank balance. We set our hearts on money and possessions not only because of greed and selfishness but also because of insecurity and anxiety. Giving breaks the power of these things over our lives. A life of generosity says loud and clear, 'I trust God to look after me.' It is to know that every hair on my head has been counted by him. To give is to find freedom.

Be like Jesus – give your life away.

Live it!

It remains an unfortunate but totally accurate truth that the last thing that often gets converted in a Christian is their bank account. Whether we hunt for excuses to keep it back for ourselves or whether we worry about not having enough, there are sadly too many of us Christians out there whose attitude to money is a lot less developed than other aspects of our relationship with God. But while the giving of our money is a vitally important part of Christianity as it shows something of our dependence, commitment and thankfulness to God, let's not fall into the trap that this is the only area in which we face the challenge of being generous. There's plenty we can do to show that we're fighting the trend for 'ME FIRST'. And this is what it's all about; making a stand, being different, refusing to go along with the flow that pushes against the standard set by God. If you want to get deep, the real problem with materialism – along with the fact that it tramples on the poor – is that it encourages people to turn their back on God. It sees us taking a fast train straight back to the Israelites who were constantly chasing after foreign gods and false idols. With wealth as our aim and guide in life we find ourselves in strange territory, far from home. Let's keep close by God, let's make sure that nothing else muscles in on his place as Lord of All in our lives.

Task 1

Use a Bible concordance to find out what the Bible has to say about money. You'll find plenty in both the Old and the New Testaments, and Proverbs has some great insight into the mind of a man who had plenty of cash to spare. Try and build up a picture of what God thinks about money. At what point does it become a problem in our lives? How can it be a good thing?

Task 2

That historical hero of eighteenth-century Christianity and co-founder of Methodism, John Wesley, decided that he would set the amount he would live on at a certain level: whatever else he earned he would give away. And he did: from when he was a young man through to the end of his life, he stuck to his financial ceiling. Are you prepared to take a similarly radical stance against the tide of greed and materialism?

Task 3

Moving on from the issue of money, is there anything else that you've got that you could be generous with? What about giving up some of your free time to volunteer at a local old people's home? Are you into washing cars, gardening, working with children or caring for the environment? Use your passions to make a difference in the world around you.

15

How to keep on going

(a chapter about persevering)

Other people always seemed to have this whole Christianity thing a good deal more sussed than me. Since I was first eased into my spiritual nappies I had a knack for checking out the person up front and thinking but one simple thought: I hate you. While they might enlighten audiences with heart-wrenching tales of personal torment and tragedy, my response would be a self-righteous, 'Pah! You think you've had it hard?' In my defence I could list numerous reasons why mine was a worse deal than theirs, although most of them came down to the simple fact that they were up there on stage, I was down in the crowd and none of it was at all fair. At the very heart of my 'confusion' was a blindness to the fact that God moves in mysterious ways, unimpressed by those things that we seem to get so hung up about (like fame and recognition), yet well into the things that we often dismiss as belonging to the bottom of the spiritual pile (like servant-heartedness and attitude).

Jesus said that he made his way down here so that we might have life and have it in all its fullness. It wasn't his intention that we spend our time limping around, enduring a second-rate existence. My problem was that I took this to mean that we were to get exactly what we wanted when we wanted. As I hope we've seen throughout this book, the life that God values is not necessarily one marked out by the glitz and glamour of our misinterpretations of success.

In a strange way my whingeing in the general direction of God and those who had 'made it in life' prevented me from actually doing anything about it. I was enjoying much the same role as the competitive father who screams from the touchlines as his youngest plays in the Under 11s five-a-side; getting out there and doing something was just not an option. Perhaps the root of it all was a mistaken belief that 'abundant life' meant an abundance of my kind of good things, when what it really means is a true and full relationship with God as father, saviour and creator of the world. Perhaps if I had worked as hard as I could to reach the goal I would have come up against another problem (one that sadly affects many more Christians than we would like to admit): the temptation to either sell out, burn out or fade out.

Our relationship with our creator is often talked about in terms of a journey. We have all been encouraged to run the race and to keep on pressing towards the prize, but just how much do we realise that we are taking part in a marathon, and not a sprint? The prize doesn't go to the person who makes the most progress in the shortest time, nor does it go to whoever falls over and barks the most. At the end of the day we will be standing face to face with God, and I want to know him as well as possible by that time. It is important that we prepare ourselves to run the marathon, to go all the way and not give up.

King David made sure that we had a top-notch example of long-term commitment and development. Through his story in the Old Testament we see great accomplishments and tremendous mistakes. Despite falling in ways that many of us can relate to, David was still described as being a man after God's heart. Despite tripping over the hurdles with such incredible style, he got up and he kept going. The key to his success? I believe that it's essentially very simple: he finished well because he started well.

Before we get on to David...

I became a Christian when I was fifteen and, as I mentioned earlier in the book, I wanted to do church work from that moment on. Between the ages of fifteen and twenty-nine there was a large gap in my life; at times I waited patiently, at other times I got annoyed. I was sure my calling was out there, there was just a small matter of getting it to me that needed to be sorted out. As a consequence I put very little into my other activities during that time. I was uninterested at school, lethargic at university and vague when I got to work. I wish now that I had done more with those years and used them in preparation for the future, whatever that was going to contain.

I know a man called James Ryle who pastors a church in Denver, Colorado. He spent his early days as a Christian a little differently to the way that I spent mine. At the time of his conversion he was serving a sentence for involuntary manslaughter as the result of a car accident in which a passenger of his died. While he was in prison he used his time to read the Bible from cover to cover, and devoured whole chunks of the dictionary to improve his vocabulary. He knew that when he got out he was going to do something to communicate the truth about Jesus to other people, just as he had found out himself. Because of his vision, he used his time wisely. It would have been easy to spend those years in jail feeling like his life was rotting away, being wasted, while he could be doing so much more with it. Today, James is still reaping the benefit of those years of disciplined preparation.

David was a little shepherd boy

In a culture where the older you were than your brothers the better, David was not off to a flying start; he was number eight of Jesse's sons. One day his family received a visit to their home in Bethlehem from the prophet Samuel. He was visiting as a result of what he believed God had told him, that one of Jesse's sons was to be anointed as the new king over Israel. Samuel told Jesse to consecrate himself and his sons and accompany him to the sacrifice.

When Jesse and his sons arrived, Samuel saw Eliab and thought to himself that he had to be the future king. It didn't occur to him that anyone other than the eldest son would be in line for the job. 'But the LORD said to Samuel, "Do not consider his appearance or his height, for I have rejected him. The LORD does not look at the things man looks at. Man looks at the outward appearance, but the LORD looks at the heart' (1 Sam. 16:7).

That happens to be one of my favourite verses in Scripture. We all do place so much value on the external appearance, judging people on all sorts of criteria from age and beauty to style and class. What God was actually saying was that his values are less superficial than ours. It is important to note that God did not reject Eliab as a person – he loved Eliab as one of his children – but as king over Israel.

The Bible goes on to say that later, after all of Jesse's sons had been presented to Samuel (and subsequently rejected), Samuel asked Jesse whether there were any more sons for him to look at. 'There is still the youngest,' Jesse answered, 'but he is tending the sheep.'

It amazes me that Jesse didn't even say his name. It was as if he thought his son's chances of ever being much more than a shepherd were so slim that he not only didn't trouble Samuel by bringing David along, but he didn't bother saying his name. So Samuel told him to send for David. When he came, the Lord told Samuel that his search was over and to anoint him at once. Imagine David – one minute he's tending his flock, then the next he finds himself anointed as king over all Israel. Then, as if none of that was strange enough, he returns to the fields where he gets on with the job of being a shepherd boy (we know this because in verse 19, after the anointing, it says, 'Then Saul sent messengers to Jesse and said, "Send me your son David, who is with the sheep."')

Call me fussy, but life as a sheep-nanny would not be my first choice to prepare me as direct ruler over all Israel; I would be keen to make sure that I was well accustomed to a life of luxury before it became an official duty. David, on the other hand, went back to his old life, carrying on as before with his boring, lonely and unnoticed job. Whenever I have been doing something that fulfils those criteria I have found it nearly impossible to resist the temptation to slack off and do something else. The temptation has been to confuse a dull, unappreciated task with a lack of spiritual kudos. Put the other way around, doing the public, esteemed jobs often seems to be so *right, so of the Lord*. Study, work and preparation may not seem related to the job of your dreams – at times being a shepherd may not have made much sense to David – but God often uses people who have prepared, calling those who have not wasted their present by whining about the future.

What did David do when he was looking after the sheep? I think he got to know his God. All the indications are that he spent those lonely nights in prayer, communicating with God and developing their relationship. The backdrop to this friendship was the raw earth, the hills and the desert. David reflects this through his psalms, writing about the God he meets in the mountains, the wind and the sky. Through contemplating the products of God's creativity and by spending time in prayer, David made sure that his time was not wasted.

Second, it seems from the Scripture that David was great on the harp. Now we may be in danger of reading a little too much into the text with this, but it isn't hard to imagine what sort of reaction David might have got from his seven elder brothers when he practised at home. This leads nicely on to the conclusion that David spent a fair amount of his scale and harmony time out in the desert. As well as music, he worked on the psalms – originally written as lyrics – and developed his talents. Again we see that his time wasn't wasted, but used wisely to hone skills that would later lead many to develop their own relationship with God.

Finally David found opportunity to put his faith into action. The all-work-and-no-play combination didn't appear to do Jack much good, and David made sure that his shepherding career wasn't just backed up by study and prayer; when he had to, David was ready to leap in and defend his flock.

The great unveiling

The story of David's encounter with Goliath reads like a grand unveiling of the David Project. He displays all the attributes on which he has diligently worked away from public view and praise. At the time, the giant was taunting his enemies, and no one in Israel would accept his challenge. David's initial task was set by his father: to take provisions to his brothers (note the liberal spread of irony with the word 'provisions' – what God provided them with, in the shape of David, was far more than they could have ever hoped for). When he arrived at the camp David was surprised to find that Goliath's threats went unanswered, and offered to resolve the situation himself. Saul's reply was to question David's age and experience in the light of the giant's 'abilities'.

What was David's knock-out answer to convince Saul and everyone else that this boy could fight this huge, hardened soldier? 'Your servant has been keeping his father's sheep.' I am not sure they would have been convinced.

He continued,

When a lion or a bear came and carried off a sheep
from the flock, I went after it, struck it and rescued the
sheep from its mouth. When it turned on me, I seized
it by its hair, struck it and killed it. Your servant has
killed both the lion and the bear; this uncircumcised
Philistine will be like one of them, because he has
defied the armies of the living God. The LORD who
delivered me from the paw of the lion and the paw of
the bear will deliver me from the hands of this
Philistine.

(1 Sam. 17:34–7)

This was David's graduation; all that he had learnt when
surrounded by sheep was clear to see. He displayed trust,
faith and wisdom beyond both his social standing and his
years. His boring, lonely and unnoticed job had taught him
well, and trained him for a conflict he could never have
predicted. Yet he knew that Goliath would be the same as a
bear or a lion; he knew because he had killed the beasts
before, and because his relationship with his creator was
deep enough to back up his hunch that what he was about
to do was right.

It would have been easy for David to wonder why he
was looking after sheep when he had been anointed as king
over Israel. Surely that made him too important to look
after a flock of sheep? Looking at our situations, we may
feel indignant that we are not at Soul Survivor, Greenbelt
or Spring Harvest, leading, teaching or entertaining the
masses with our own gifting. Perhaps we may feel that as
our place is on stage, we won't busy ourselves with those
menial tasks that people who don't get up on the stage
have to do. Time and time again people have discovered
that God, like a wise father, trusts people with the small
things before he moves them on to the bigger ones.

David learnt his lessons well, despite the fact that he

must have wondered how God was going to engineer a career change from shepherd boy to reigning monarch. It seems slightly unlikely that his 'to do' list contained the instruction 'practise slaying large animals just in case I ever meet a big Philistine'. *His* task was to be faithful in the small, to be obedient in a present that seemed divorced from ambition. As he lived his own life, God made sure that he received a full preparation for an unpredictable future. Like David, we could do well to learn not to waste the moment, to express our love for Jesus by serving him when there is nobody around to watch. If we can learn to deliver the goods when ours is an audience of one, if we can learn to value the approval of God more than that of other people, then it will be immaterial whether we are seen by ten or ten thousand.

Enjoy the silence

Maybe there is a reason why so many of us cry out for company: perhaps the presence of pain and hurt inside demands the presence of people around us, taking the focus away from what we need to deal with and placing it on others. I spent a long time avoiding issues buried deep within by never really being alone. I knew that there would be considerable pain waiting for me when I turned up, but it would only be when I was alone and facing things that God could help me. Many of David's psalms reflect the solitude of his job, and many echo the cry that comes from deep within us when we are faced with pain: where are you, God? It is a great thing to have fellowship, to hang out with and enjoy time with others, and something we need to do, but not as a substitute for spending time with God, in solitude, allowing him to search us and find anything that does not reflect his purity.

This is the bit where I risk sounding like a very old and dull person, but life can sometimes be boring – it was for

David and it is for us. The temptation is to confuse mono-
tony with a lack of spirituality (this job is dull so God can't
be in it) and to equate those gooey rushes of emotion with
an abundance of it (I fell over seventeen times at church
today and it was great). The quest for a deeper relationship
with God and the quest for a more explosive encounter with
him are travelling in two separate directions. To hanker for
one high after another will result in a crisis of disillu-
sionment when the realisation hits that God likes us close,
attentive and obedient. We need to learn to stick things out,
because perseverance comes very high on the list of things
that God loves, choosing as he does to develop many things
in us through it.

James 1:2 is a favourite verse of mine, carrying the
immortal message that we should 'Consider it pure joy . . .
[to] face trials of many kinds because you know that the
testing of your faith develops perseverance.' I have seen
loads of people who started well, who had plenty of gifts
and anointing, but have fallen by the wayside simply because they have not known how to keep going. They
thought that they had signed up for a 100-metre sprint, but
then they found out that they were in a marathon. I have
seen others who at the beginning were fairly unimpressive
from the outside, yet kept plodding on in their relationship
with God. Such training has produced strong and healthy
Christians.

The power of the plodder

Friends of mine once asked Steve Chalke what he thought
his greatest asset was. I was fairly sure that his personality,
broadcasting experience or looks would come pretty high
on the list. He really shocked me when he said, 'I'm a
plodder. Whether things are good or bad, I just keep going.'

I remember hearing someone say once that God is not
looking so much for great ability in us, or even credibility

with others, but for our availability to him. We need to learn to be available to him all the time. God looks not for super-stars but for servants. He looks for people who will follow him, as long as it takes and wherever it goes.

I am a great, true and genuine supporter of Manchester United. It is well known by my friends that I can recite the line-up since 1973, and often like to practise this among them on long journeys. I read an interview with David Beckham in which he was asked what he thought it was that had made him a Premier League player. Like the man himself, the answer was short yet totally accurate: practice. As a child he would spend hours kicking a ball against a wall or playing with his dad. We too need to practise, we need to give our spirituality the chance to develop from clumsy infancy to skilled adulthood. We need to seek God with all that we have, especially when there appears to be nothing in it for us, except him.

At the beginning of this book we talked about worship, which is the search for God. We want to finish by saying that to truly live the life is to pursue God with all our lives, following him with everything that we have, obeying him in the most menial and unnoticed of tasks. Our spiritual life is meant to be like an iceberg; the visible tip should be 10 per cent of what is below the surface of the water. We would do well to develop the 90 per cent of our lives before God and God only. Through that exercise of perseverance comes righteousness and a deeper relationship with God. That way, later on in life when prosperity comes to us in marriage or a career, we won't sell out to the world because we will have been trained to value the completion of the race more highly than the view along the way. Likewise we won't burn out. We will pace ourselves, learn to keep going, to see it through to the end. We won't fade out like those who start well but whose enthusiasm for God gradually dims. Ours will be a spirituality that perseveres.

Live it!

A tricky one. So many Christians seem to burn out, get tired or, worse, disillusioned when things don't seem to go their own way. But you know, I reckon there's a strong case for arguing that Christianity does follow some fairly basic natural patterns; I know that my life is a mixed bag of seasons where I feel closer to God than at other times as well as periods where I feel as though I'm totally on fire for God, alongside those where the feelings are numbed and dulled. Perhaps what really matters is that, while we learn to take notice of the way we feel, we don't fall into the trap of allowing our feelings to be our sole guide in our relationship with God. Think of it like a marriage: it's not all high-octane romance twenty-four hours a day, and the best marriages I know are the ones where both partners are committed to each other for the long haul, whether they feel all gooey or not. Let's not get into the position where we think it's OK to go cold on God, get bored with him and treat him like a fashion accessory. God is eternal. He is true. He is almighty. And he is all those things whether we feel it or not.

But where do you go from here? How does this affect your life on a practical level? Well, like a good marriage, having a relationship with God means signing up for three things: communication, communication and communication. That means taking time out to pray, to tell God how you are feeling, to commit your whole life to him, to confess and repent of the things you have done wrong, to draw close to him in intimacy, giving him the sacrifice of praise that he deserves. And it means being open to the communication that comes from the other direction as well: learning to hear the promptings of the Holy Spirit as you go about your day, hearing him speak to you as you look to exercise the gift of prophecy, learning to get to know the thousands of words inspired by God and written in the Bible, hearing the still, small voice that echoes on the winds of creation.

Task 1

Experiment with different formats for your 'quiet time'. Try having it at different times, in different places, using different resources and varying the format. Some of us love routines, but there are others who get bored when we feel that things are getting stale. Get to know yourself and mould your approach to play to your strengths.

Task 2

Read Richard Forster's fantastic book *Celebration of Discipline* – don't worry, it's not a greatest hits of torture techniques.